Table of Contents

Appendices

Appendix A: Key Terms & Definitions

Appendix B: Creative Financing Strategies at a Glance

Appendix C: International Real Estate Investment Considerations

Appendix D: Recommended Resources

Appendix E: Sample Contracts & Forms

Appendix F: Common Myths & Misconceptions

Glossary

Bibliography

of the use of the information contained within this document, including, but not limited to, errors, omissions, or inaccuracies.

ISBN: 978-1-967690-01-5

Foreword

Real estate has long been one of the most powerful vehicles for wealth creation, offering financial freedom, stability, and generational wealth opportunities. Yet, for many aspiring investors, traditional financing requirements rigid lending criteria, high down payments, and strict credit score thresholds make property ownership feel like an impossible goal. The good news? Those barriers are not absolute. With the proper knowledge and strategies, anyone can unlock doors that seem closed, leveraging creative financing to transform obstacles into stepping stones.

That's where Creative Financing comes in.

Dr. John Workman has created a definitive guide that goes beyond conventional investment wisdom. He doesn't just focus on how to finance real estate deals he teaches you how to think like an investor, identifying opportunities where others see roadblocks. Investors can build and scale their portfolios without relying solely on banks by leveraging seller financing, lease options, private lending, and other innovative strategies. But the power of creative financing isn't limited to domestic markets it extends globally.

Real estate investing is no longer confined by borders. The rise of international markets, digital transactions, and global financing options means that investors today have access to a wealth of opportunities beyond their home countries.

Whether it's securing properties in emerging economies, diversifying assets across stable foreign markets, or leveraging international financing structures, Creative Financing equips you with the tools to expand your portfolio worldwide. Dr. Workman skillfully explores how investors can navigate foreign markets, assess risks, and leverage creative funding to take advantage of lucrative international deals.

This book is more than just a manual it's a mindset shift. The real estate game is evolving, and those who succeed are not necessarily those with the deepest pockets but those with the sharpest strategies. Whether you're a first-time investor or a seasoned professional looking to break into international real estate, the insights in this book will empower you to think globally, act strategically, and build a real estate empire on your own terms. If you're ready to embrace innovative financing solutions and expand your horizons both financially and geographically Creative Financing will serve as your ultimate guide.

Turn the page. The world is your market.
John Workman, Ph.D.

Dedication

To my mother, Sallie M. Workman,

Your strength, resilience, and unwavering love shaped the foundation of my life. As a single mother, you carried the immense responsibility of raising six sons, instilling in us the values of perseverance, hard work, and integrity. Though you never owned a home yourself, the seeds you planted in us grew into a legacy of homeownership, financial wisdom, and the pursuit of more significant opportunities.

This book is a testament to the lessons you taught not through words alone, but through the sacrifices you made and the example you set. You showed me that true wealth isn't measured in possessions but in the love we share, the strength we carry, and the dreams we dare to pursue.

With deepest gratitude and love, I dedicate this book to you. Your journey paved the way for me, and for that, I am forever grateful.

With love,
Your son, Johnny

Epigraph

"Wealth isn't built by waiting for the perfect opportunity it's built by creating it. The key to success in real estate isn't just money; it's strategy, creativity, and the courage to move when others hesitate."

John Workman, Ph.D.

Introduction

In a world where financial security often feels elusive, the quest for independence drives many to explore new avenues of wealth generation. Real estate investment has emerged as a compelling option, offering not only the promise of potential profit but also a sense of control over one's financial future. Yet, the barriers to entry can seem daunting. This book aims to demystify those hurdles and offer you a roadmap to success through creative financing a method that has empowered countless individuals to achieve their real estate dreams without traditional constraints.

Imagine being able to build a real estate empire without the immediate need for substantial cash reserves or conventional loans. Creative financing methods unlock previously inaccessible opportunities, which enable swift property acquisitions and investment growth. This book offers essential knowledge and tools to both real estate newcomers and seasoned investors who want innovative strategies to tackle market complexities with confidence.

Throughout history, real estate has been a proven path to building wealth. However, in today's ever-evolving financial landscape, new methods are required to stay ahead. The traditional approaches, marked by rigid lending criteria and hefty down payments, may no longer be viable options for everyone. Here, creativity meets pragmatism as we delve into the various financing techniques that prioritize flexibility and innovation. Utilizing these strategies lets you lower risk exposure while boosting returns and enables you to acquire properties that would typically be considered inaccessible.

Our objective is clear: We aim to provide you with basic real estate investment knowledge and showcase essential concepts and strategies that lead to successful investing. You'll discover practical skills to analyze and evaluate investment opportunities effectively, ensuring each decision builds towards your long-term goals. While the financial realm is notorious for its complex jargon, this book strives to simplify terms and offer actionable advice, making it accessible even to those taking their first steps into the world of property investment.

A critical aspect of real estate investing is knowing where to begin and how to make knowledgeable judgments that align with both short-term needs and long-term aspirations. Through this book, you'll learn about some of the best creative financing techniques available. We'll explore options like seller financing, lease options, and partnerships each method tailored to overcome specific financial roadblocks. By understanding these strategies, you'll be better prepared to assess rental properties for cash flow, leveraging the resources and tools required for effective decision-making.

Financial freedom represents more than an aspiration because it functions as a lifestyle choice that provides security and enables wealth-building while promoting empowerment. Take charge of your financial future by developing a growth-oriented mindset that focuses on lifelong learning and ongoing progress. From navigating career demands and family obligations to pursuing personal development and networking, our lifestyles reflect our values and priorities. This book aligns with those values, providing pragmatic solutions that are both time-efficient and cost-effective.

As you embark on this journey, it's essential to recognize the power of community. When you work together with peers and mentors as well as investor groups, you gain improved experience through shared knowledge, tips, and support. You can avoid isolation when investing in real estate by engaging with others. By collaborating with other investors who share similar goals, you can build a network that enriches both personal and professional growth.

Ultimately, this book speaks to the driven and goal-oriented individuals who approach challenges with enthusiasm and a positive outlook. While skeptical of promises that sound too good to be true, you're open-minded enough to explore new methods if they show potential value. Risk-aware yet informed, you're willing to take calculated steps to secure a stable future, motivated by the desire to generate reliable passive income streams, expand your portfolio, and leave a legacy.

Addressing common concerns, such as lack of initial knowledge, financing apprehensions, and market complexity, this book provides structured, step-by-step guidance designed to boost your confidence and accelerate your path to success. By the end of this manuscript, you'll possess a comprehensive toolkit empowering you to make strategic financial choices that align with your financial objectives.

Whether you're seeking to enter the real estate arena with minimal upfront capital or looking to refine your existing strategies, this guide offers something for everyone. It positions itself as a beacon of clarity amidst the intricate world of real estate financing, paving the way for informed and inspired action.

So, prepare to commence on a transformative journey. With the right knowledge, mindset, and strategies, achieving financial independence via real estate is not just a possibility it's well within your grasp. This book serves as your companion, mentor, and motivator, helping you navigate the exciting landscape of real estate investment with optimism and determination. Welcome to a future of unlimited potential.

Ch. 1 - Creative Financing Fundamentals

Real estate investors benefit from creative financing because it offers adaptable methods that extend beyond traditional lending practices. Real estate investors who choose non-traditional financing options find it easier to engage in property transactions when they cannot obtain traditional loans. Non-traditional financing options turn roadblocks into opportunities, especially for people who fail to meet standard mortgage requirements. Both new investors and those looking to grow their investment portfolios can discover untapped potential by examining creative financing options, which will push them to think outside traditional methods.

This chapter looks into the fundamental theory that authenticates creative financing options in the real estate market. This segment provides knowledge about seller financing and lease options, which are adaptable financial solutions for various circumstances. We will highlight the requirements of detailed due diligence and proper legal documentation as protective measures against the potential risks associated with non-traditional strategies. Understanding the adaptability of these strategies in response to economic changes and market volatility positions you to handle real estate complexities better. This journey will enlarge your knowledge base while at the same time enforcing your decision-making skills to fully use creative financing methods when it comes to your investment strategies.

Defining Creative Financing:

Creative financing represents a revolutionary approach to real estate that employs unconventional financial strategies to surpass established funding techniques. Non-traditional financing methods, including seller financing and lease options, create additional transaction opportunities for buyers and sellers who might be unable to participate through standard methods. Individuals with insufficient capital or those facing difficulties with traditional bank loan requirements benefit significantly from this approach.

The stringent credit score requirements and large down payments demanded by traditional lenders create financial obstacles for new investors and early portfolio builders seeking investment opportunities. Customized strategies from alternative financing options help break through existing barriers by tailoring solutions to each party's unique situation.

The property owner takes on the lender's position and offers financial support directly to the buyer in seller financing. Seller financing allows buyers to pay monthly installments directly to the property owner instead of a bank, which lets people who fail to obtain traditional loans complete property transactions. Buyers use lease options to rent a property with the intention of buying it later while using this period to improve their credit scores or gather enough funds. Flexible financial strategies enable buyers who would usually be rejected by traditional lenders to proceed with their purchases.

A logical question to ask would be, "What reasons would drive a seller to sign a seller's agreement?" Properties located in non-traditional neighborhoods with distinctive features can remain unsold longer than predicted because traditional lending requirements limit buyer interest. To avoid endless delays from waiting for a bank-approved buyer, sellers can decide to provide their own financing. A homeowner might encounter difficulties selling their property through traditional methods because the lack of nearby comparable homes causes lenders to doubt loan approvals. The owner can attract more prospective buyers through seller financing since it appeals to motivated buyers who struggle to meet standard credit or down payment requirements. The seller receives regular payments that usually carry higher interest rates, providing protection against potential risks. This setup accelerates the sale procedure by granting sellers authority over repayment schedules, which helps them to match buyer expectations with their own financial security. This sales technique remains unknown to most sellers, which surprises many people.

A significant number of sellers who could gain from this technique overlook its potential as an option. The development of creative financing methods stemmed partly from significant economic shifts and financial system crises (Malaysia | Mercer Learning). The 2008 financial crisis triggered a risk assessment reevaluation, which led to the development of more adaptable financing methods as individuals looked for mortgage market alternatives (Mehta, 2023). When credit became tighter, and cautiousness increased, non-traditional financing became an enduring strategy that enabled investors to manage market downturns effectively.

Creative financing methods offer several advantages, but their risks require diligent oversight due to their non-standard nature. Investors can minimize potential disputes by performing extensive due diligence combined with legally compliant documentation practices. Participants in these varied agreements must understand their duties right from the start because of their complex structures. Transparency prevents misunderstandings while at the same time ensuring adherence to legal standards.

A complete risk management approach is needed to stay informed about current market trends alongside legal standards. The constant changes in real estate laws make it essential to seek guidance from seasoned real estate brokers, attorneys, and financial advisors. Professional advisors deliver insights into both federal and local regulations and identify potential legal issues while assisting in the development of safeguarding contracts. Whether it is for buyers or sellers, knowledge and professional guidance are crucial to creating a secure and advantageous deal (Creative Financing: Real Estate, Strategies, Types, Examples, 2023).

Throughout history, non-traditional financing methods have proven their ability to adapt and remain stable over time. The introduction of new regulations and economic changes led mainstream banks to modify their policies, and this shift drove the development of creative financing solutions that served as alternatives to conventional, restrictive lending methods. New and seasoned real estate professionals both started to identify these methods as necessary tools for investors seeking non-traditional funding options.

Creative financing offers numerous advantages but requires navigation through various distinct challenges. Investors need to carefully assess the unique benefits and drawbacks that each financing approach provides. Seller financing can make it easier to own property by extending the payment period of the loans term. But it can also increase the risk of the buyers not being able to make their payments due to the longer term. Applying non-traditional financial methods requires strategic thinking that integrates risk and reward management, thorough planning, and continuous market awareness.

The key to success lies in understanding how risks correlate with potential rewards (Planning Archives - ANDREW PURDIE). Investors who utilize creative financing approaches need to keep an open mind about unusual solutions and adjust their strategies according to changing market conditions (Unlocking Cash Flow: How Invoice Factoring Benefits Businesses). By combining meticulous planning with exact execution, they can discover investment opportunities that traditional lending methods fail to reveal.

Importance of Creative Financing in Real Estate:

Real estate investors implement innovative financing methods to bypass the limitations presented by standard lending mechanisms. Traditional banks enforce stringent requirements for loan approval, which include maintaining good credit standing and providing extensive financial documentation along with substantial down payment commitments. These barriers present obstacles that can hinder new investors, those who are self-employed, and those wanting to quickly grow their investment portfolios. Investors can utilize creative financing to access flexible funding solutions that align with their specific financial requirements and investment goals.

Creative financing stands out for its ability to navigate capital restrictions and credit obstacles. Investors without adequate savings for significant down payments can turn to hard money loans, which depend on property assets instead of a buyer's credit history. In contrast to traditional banks, which assess borrowers' debt-to-income ratios (to be discussed later) and financial backgrounds, hard money lenders base their lending decisions on property value, which enables investors with poor credit to obtain financing.

Expanding Investment Opportunities with Alternative Financing:

Investors gain access to otherwise unattainable properties through the use of alternative financial arrangements. Such alternative financing methods like seller financing, lease options, private money lending, and subject-to-financing, investors can bypass banks and discover new ways to structure their deals. Buyers can get more advantageous loan conditions by conversing directly with property owners through seller financing, such as lower interest rates and decreased initial payments. Lease options offer investors a secure method to get involved with real estate ownership, which allows them to benefit financially before finalizing their purchase. Creative financing methods become particularly important in competitive real estate markets where cash buyers (who usually want to pay well below market value) are prevalent, and standard buyers cannot secure traditional loans.

The primary characteristic of creative financing lies in its ability to adapt to different situations. Direct negotiations between buyers and sellers result in agreements that can close faster than traditional loans, which in turn speeds up property transactions in a competitive real estate markets. During this period, structured contracts such as lease options enable buyers to develop their creditworthiness while locking in a predetermined purchase price. These personalized solutions allow investors to make informed decisions and secure strategic advantages in dynamic market conditions.

Here is how it would work. A couple looking for their first home faces financial obstacles that bar them from obtaining a standard mortgage in their competitive housing market. The property owner suggests a lease option to the couple because they know the couple wants to buy the property. Under this agreement, the couple enters a lease that allows them to buy the home at a predetermined price within a defined timeframe but at the same time the agreement does not force them to make the purchase. The couple allocates some of their monthly rent payment towards building a down payment fund during the lease period while they work on improving their credit score and financial stability. Their goal is to improve their qualification to purchase the property at a later date. On the other side of the equation, the seller receives consistent income along with the possibility of realizing a sale opportunity. This method enables buyers to obtain a secure route to owning a home that may have been inaccessible to them initially. When done correctly, this technique presents a win-win situation for both the buyer and the seller. The buyer can obtain the property where, under traditional conditions, they cannot. The seller gets the chance to sell the property, and in the event the buyers change their mind, the signup fee that the buyer pays and the higher rent is retained by the seller (The essential factors).

Overcoming Credit Barriers:

Investors who need to rebuild or establish their credit find creative financing solutions appealing because traditional lenders place immense importance on credit scores. Lease option participants start with a rental period, which gives them time to build a better credit score before buying the property. Buyers benefit from this incremental approach because it enables them to bypass early limitations and pursue property ownership according to their planned financial timeline.

For instance, a low credit score prevented Alex from being eligible for a traditional mortgage after spending years renting and wanting to own a home. Banks continued to label him as a high-risk borrower despite his stable income and consistent debt repayments because previous financial problems had damaged his credit report. The repeated loan rejections drove Alex to look for other ways to buy a home and led him to find out about the lease option strategy.

Alex entered into a lease-option agreement through a real estate investor, which permitted him to rent a house with a purchase option available after a two-year period. The deal locked his purchase price so he would not face higher costs if property values rose before, he made his purchase. A part of his monthly rental payments during the lease period went toward his upcoming down payment. During this time, Alex rebuilt his credit by making timely payments and reducing his debt while enhancing his financial status.

Alex improved his credit score significantly during the two-year lease period, which allowed him to meet mortgage eligibility requirements. By maintaining regular lease payments, he built a dependable financial history, which made lenders view him as a lower-risk borrower. Alex used his option fee and rent credits to fund his down payment, which helped him secure a mortgage with favorable interest rates to become a homeowner. The step-by-step nature of the lease option enabled him to surmount initial credit limitations. He purchased his house at his desired speed while building his financial stability over time.

Diversifying Funding Sources:

Non-traditional investment approaches enable seasoned investors to expand their portfolios without too much dependence on traditional debt options. Home equity loans, crowdfunding, and subject-to-financing enable investors to explore various funding opportunities that offer specific benefits. An investor could secure a home equity line of credit (HELOC) to expand their property portfolio without selling current assets and utilize crowdfunding to raise funds from multiple investors to participate in large-scale projects.

A range of financing options enables risk reduction through distribution across multiple instruments while allowing investors to adjust to changing market conditions (Vaughns, S. (2012)). People can develop custom investment approaches for short-term profits and sustainable growth by using both standard and alternative financing methods.

Investors aiming to benefit from these opportunities should commit time to studying different creative financing methods. Engaging with experienced professionals and finding mentors helps investors deepen their understanding and prevent common errors. Negotiations achieve mutually advantageous terms through the essential practice of open disclosure of financial capacity and objectives.

The complexities of current approaches create a need for investors to monitor both their legal responsibilities and financial commitments. Both parties benefit from understanding their obligations when legal professionals assess contracts to establish a reliable foundation for business success. Thorough research of both local and federal laws empowers buyers and sellers with increased protection from legal problems and troublesome contracts.

Common Myths and Realities:

The implementation of creative financing methods in real estate often encounters problems because of misunderstandings between parties. By being able to separate reality from misconceptions, investors gain the knowledge required to choose wisely and apply non-traditional financing strategies with assured understanding.

Myth #1: Creative financing is for desperate investors only.

Reality: Successful real estate moguls have expanded their asset portfolios for years by utilizing non-traditional financial tools, such as lease options or seller financing, to maintain minimal capital allocation (Creative Financing and Some Things to Know, 2025).

Myth #2: Non-traditional financing is riskier than conventional loans.

Reality: All investments carry risk. Through meticulous market research combined with comprehensive agreements and expert legal counsel, creative financing achieves equal stability and profitability compared to conventional methods (PodBean Development, 2023). Investors who use multiple financing approaches will lower their susceptibility to unexpected market changes.

Myth #3: Creative financing lacks regulation and reliability.

Reality: Some creative financing agreements require customization, but many operate under more established legal frameworks that protect both parties (Creative Financing and Some Things to Know, 2025). Getting expert attorneys and trustworthy financiers ensures that unconventional transactions meet legal standards, which enhances investor trust and validates the transaction process.

Myth #4: Economic downturns undermine creative financing.

Reality: When the economy slows down, or lenders impose tight restrictions, non-traditional financing approaches experience growth. Investors who used seller financing or lease options remained able to close deals during the 2008 credit crunch, while traditional banks restricted lending (Mehta, 2023). These strategies remain effective under economic stress and provide essential support when conventional financing options disappear.

Myth #5: Creative financing does not include private or hard money loans.

Reality: Private and hard money loans qualify as creative financing solutions because they offer quick approval processes and flexible terms despite their higher interest rates (Creative Financing and Some Things to Know, 2025). Such loans might not suit every scenario, but they allow investors to quickly capitalize on time-sensitive changes.

People who are dubious about exploring these financing options should seek guidance through educational resources and mentorship. Case studies, along with success stories and expert insights provided by real estate clubs, workshops, and online forums, work to dismantle misconceptions. The cooperative approach reduces recognized financial risks and inspires shared learning, which makes creative financing accessible to a great many individuals (PodBean Development, 2023)

Summary and Reflections:

Real estate creative financing provides access to opportunities that are beyond the reach of traditional loan options. By using alternative methods such as seller financing and subject-to-deals, investors bypass conventional lending limitations. New investors without significant funds and established investors seeking portfolio expansion through diversification benefit from these adaptable financing strategies.

Creative financing provides people with control over their fiscal path through the strategic transformation of challenges into opportunities. Exploring unconventional strategies with thorough preparation and expert advice creates a solid basis for confidently navigating the market. When managed responsibly, these techniques provide immediate access to profitable opportunities and develop a sustainable foundation for enduring growth and prosperity.

Malaysia | Mercer Learning - Fundamentals of Compensation And Rewards Analytics Using Excel.

Planning Archives - ANDREW PURDIE.

Unlocking Cash Flow: How Invoice Factoring Benefits Businesses | TopMarketWatch.com.

Vaughns, S. (2012). Open innovation implementation: Competitor pathways.

The essential factors followed by house-buying companies – Gio Music. https://giomusic.net/the-essential-factors-followed-by-house-buying-companies/

Ch. 2 - Leveraging Equity in Real Estate

Investors who look to apply equity in real estate have discovered it to be a very effective strategy when it comes to boosting financial growth and achieving stability. Defining equity as just the difference between property market value and mortgage debt does not fully capture its more profound significance in making strategic investment decisions. When investors understand and manage equity correctly, it becomes a powerful mechanism for portfolio expansion and loan negotiation while providing protection from market volatility. This chapter explores the measurement and cultivation of equity, along with its potential rewards and risks, to provide you with the essential knowledge needed for making strategic decisions about utilizing your existing assets. Understanding equity basics prepares real estate investors to diversify holdings or seek financing for upcoming ventures strategically.

Understanding Equity and Its Measurement:

Equity represents the percentage of your property that you truly own after accounting for any debts secured against it. When you first purchase a home or investment property, your down payment establishes an initial share of equity. As you make regular mortgage payments particularly toward the principal you gradually build more equity. Market factors can also amplify this process: if property values appreciate over time, your equity rises in tandem. To calculate equity, you generally subtract the remaining mortgage balance from the property's current market value (Chen, 2022). For instance, if your home is valued at $300,000 and you owe $200,000, then you have $100,000 in equity. This figure is not a fixed constant; it moves with real estate market trends, regional economic conditions, and your ongoing mortgage payments.

Distinguishing between "equity" and "market value" is critical. Market value refers to how much a buyer would likely pay for the property at a given moment a figure that may rise or fall based on local demand and broader economic shifts. Equity, on the other hand, is your personal stake or ownership in the property. This is influenced by how much of the property you have paid off, any improvements you have made, and any changes to local real estate prices. Understanding this distinction helps you pinpoint what you truly own versus what you still owe.

There are several key elements that influence equity growth. Steady mortgage repayments are typically the simplest way to increase your percentage of ownership in a property, as each payment towards the principal adds to your ownership share. However, make note that your payment in the beginning will largely go toward paying the interest on the loan. As time progresses, more and more of your payment will go towards paying down the principal. Meanwhile, property improvements whether minor upgrades like painting and landscaping or significant renovations such as adding a new room can boost market value and, by extension, your equity.

Favorable market conditions can drive up property values throughout a neighborhood or region, which results in increased equity for every homeowner in that locality.

Two essential tools enable the precise evaluation of your equity position. Professional appraisals objectively assess your property's worth in today's market. An appraiser evaluates factors like the property's condition, recent sales of similar homes (comparables), and overall market trends to determine a figure to calculate equity (Equity in Real Estate Definition - Real Estate License Wizard, 2022). Second, the Loan-to-Value Ratio (LTV) measures how much of your property's worth a lender is financing, comparing the loan amount to the appraised value. A lower LTV indicates higher equity and typically grants access to more favorable loan terms.

Now that we have established how equity is calculated and measured, let us explore how you can actively grow this vital resource. You can actively put into place strategies to both grow and safeguard your existing equity instead of just relying on market gains alone.

Building Equity Through Strategic Actions:

Equity growth often begins with the market trends. The observation of regional economic indicators, including employment shifts and infrastructure advancements, can expose potential property buying opportunities before price increases occur. Investors who anticipate shifts, such as the revival of a formerly overlooked neighborhood, can gain equity quickly if the area's desirability climbs, driving up home values.

Beyond capitalizing on market trends, you can build equity by investing in upgrades. Renovations that improve the property's functionality or appeal like modernized kitchens, energy-efficient appliances, or well-maintained landscaping tend to raise market value. These enhancements not only attract prospective buyers willing to pay a premium but also can command higher rent in the case of income-generating properties. Over time, the incremental rise in your property's value directly translates into an equity boost.

Financing choices can also accelerate equity gains. For instance, refinancing at a lower interest rate frees up more of your monthly mortgage payment, which can go toward principal reduction. This approach helps you pay down your mortgage faster, effectively converting more of your house's value into your own asset. When using this technique, be aware of two things. First, make sure your mortgage does not have a pre-payment penalty. Secondly, when making that additional payment, be sure to stipulate that the extra funds within the mortgage payment are to be applied to the principal only. In most cases, when prepaying towards the principal, it is better to write a separate prepayment check with your usual mortgage payment. Staying informed about interest rate fluctuations lets you act quickly when refinancing opportunities align with your financial goals.

Regular maintenance plays a pivotal role, too. Even small issues leaky faucets, peeling paint, minor roof damage can grow into expensive problems if left unaddressed. By proactively tending to upkeep, you not only preserve property value but also safeguard the equity you have already built. The market value of a property increases when prospective buyers and lenders assess well-maintained homes positively.

Through data-driven analysis, you can determine whether to maintain your current holdings or make adjustments. A property's financial success can be gauged by key performance indicators, which include cap rates for rental properties and occupancy rates. Cap rate, or capitalization rate, is a commonly used metric to help investors evaluate the profitability of a rental property (The CAP Rate). It is calculated by dividing the property's net operating income (NOI) which accounts for expenses like maintenance, property taxes, and insurance by the property's purchase price or current market value (Hubler | AI-enabled No-Code Platform). For example, if a rental generates $10,000 in NOI annually and is valued at $100,000, it would have a cap rate of 10%. A higher cap rate suggests a potentially more lucrative return on investment, though it may also indicate more significant risk. Conversely, a lower cap rate might reflect steadier (but possibly smaller) returns and reduced risk. Investors can better gauge which opportunities align with their financial objectives and risk tolerance by considering cap rates across different properties or markets.

If a property underperforms consistently, you might consider selling it potentially capturing the equity you have built and redirecting those funds into an investment with more substantial long-term returns. After growing and preserving equity through these proactive measures, the next step is exploring how to tap into that resource without jeopardizing your financial stability. Leveraging equity carefully can open doors to fresh opportunities but also carries inherent risks that require strategic planning.

Equity as Financial Leverage - Opportunities and Risks:

Investors who utilize their accumulated equity can obtain financing for additional acquisitions, which helps them expand and diversify their real estate portfolios. A homeowner who has reduced their mortgage balance substantially in an appreciating market can tap into their property's equity to finance additional rental investments or renovations that increase property value. This reinvestment strategy can help build a robust property portfolio without waiting to save cash for a full down payment. The average down payment on an investment property can range anywhere from 20% to 25%. In some markets, that cost can be astronomical. For example, in my market, which is New York City, 25% down on an average single-family home would be in the $175,000 range.

Home equity loans and home equity lines of credit (HELOCs) are standard vehicles for accessing this built-up value (2023 Home Improvement Loans

101, Columbian). Typically, they offer competitive interest rates and relatively straightforward application processes. By converting equity into spendable capital, you tap into the money "locked" in your property. The Loan-to-Value (LTV) ratio plays an essential role here: lenders generally prefer borrowers with lower LTV, as it signals a secure equity cushion. Here is how LTV works. Suppose you own a home valued at $300,000 and have an existing mortgage of $180,000 (Rocket Homes). This means your current equity is $120,000 (the difference between the home's value and what you owe). If you take out a $50,000 home equity loan, your total debt on the property will rise to $230,000. Dividing $230,000 by the home's $300,000 value gives a Loan-to-Value (LTV) ratio of roughly 77%. Many lenders use an LTV threshold for instance, 80% when assessing risk. Maintaining an LTV below that threshold (80%) often indicates sufficient equity to secure more favorable loan terms. For you, that means greater loan flexibility and potentially better financing terms.

However, overextending through debt often referred to as over-leveraging can lead to serious financial pitfalls. Should property values decline due to broader economic slowdowns or localized market corrections, highly leveraged owners risk owing more on their properties than they are worth. The mortgage crisis of 2008 served as a stark reminder of this vulnerability; many homeowners found themselves underwater on their loans when property values plummeted (Mehta, 2023). A balanced approach to using equity can mitigate this danger. Before borrowing, investors should consider their personal risk tolerance, monthly cash flow, and the reliability of any rental income streams. Especially the reliability of rental income because even if the market moves your property value below water, the rental income from the property should remain the same and will continue to support the mortgage regardless of the fall in property value. Of course, this takes into consideration that you have put strong and reliable tenants into place.

Maintaining a level of liquidity such as a reserved emergency fund can shield you from mortgage payment shocks or sudden vacancy issues. Investments in properties or enhancements that offer dependable returns enhances your ability to handle debt obligations responsibly. Equity funds can be used to improve property features, which further boosts property value growth. The installation of a second bathroom, together with energy-efficient upgrades, enables property owners to demand higher rental prices or achieve better resale value. I had a client who was selling their home and decided to repaint the home's exterior for $5000. By doing this, he converted his home into one of the best-looking houses on the block. By doing that, he was able to increase the sale price of his house by $30,000. In this way, the money borrowed against existing equity feeds back into the property, potentially resulting in a net gain if well planned.

Employing leverage effectively requires attentive monitoring. Tracking local real estate trends, economic factors, and personal financial metrics like debt-to-income ratio can help you recognize when it is wise to leverage more and when it may be prudent to hold back. In doing so, you ensure that equity remains a strategic asset rather than a source of undue exposure (How Managed IT Services Helps Cost Optimization in the Cloud | AffinityMSP).

Final Insights:

Equity extends beyond property ownership representation because it serves as an ever-changing resource with substantial influence on real estate success. This asset can be cultivated and leveraged by monitoring market trends while keeping properties well-maintained and upgraded through strategic refinancing and home equity loans. A prudent approach to managing leverage risks protects your capital and long-term investment goals.

While working towards financial freedom, treat equity as your ultimate target and a conduit to additional possibilities. Your understanding of equity measurement and responsible capitalization provides a strong financial foundation. Your focus on either reinvesting in existing properties, acquiring new ones, or saving equity for unforeseen circumstances will help you confidently make well-informed decisions, regardless of market conditions.

The CAP Rate - New Branch Real Estate Advisors.

https://newbranchre.com/the-cap-rate/

Hubler | AI-enabled No-Code Platform.

(2023). Home improvement loans 101. Columbian, (), E.3.

How Managed IT Services Helps Cost Optimization in the Cloud | AffinityMSP.

How To Budget For House Maintenance Costs | Rocket Homes. https://www.rockethomes.com/blog/homeowner-tips/house-maintenance-cost

Ch. 3 - Navigating Mortgages for Creative Deals

You can dramatically transform your real estate investment journey by utilizing flexible financing options to acquire mortgages for creative deals. The right lending solutions will let you simplify your real estate buying process while allowing your portfolio to grow more effectively and, at the same time, increase your wealth (DNCU | Mortgage Loans Explained). This chapter examines how strategic mortgage management transforms the investment paths of both novice and experienced investors by leading them toward financial independence. Through the strategic alignment of loans with your goals and maintaining an informed mindset, you will reduce risks and increase returns, which are essential components for building long-term success.

Throughout this chapter, you'll discover various mortgage types designed to meet diverse real estate goals. We'll compare fixed-rate versus adjustable-rate loans under the conventional mortgage umbrella, illustrate how FHA and VA loans can open doors for buyers with particular needs, and discuss alternatives supporting non-traditional transactions. You'll also learn what steps to take in securing the most favorable terms such as preparing thorough documentation and becoming pre-approved while understanding how interest rate fluctuations affect your investment decisions. To round out the conversation, we explore unconventional routes like seller financing and hard money loans, highlighting how these can be harnessed strategically. At the conclusion of this chapter, you will possess the skills necessary to maneuver through changing market conditions and select mortgage products that suit your risk profile and investment objectives.

Understanding Different Mortgage Types:

Mastering creative real estate transactions begins with understanding all available mortgage choices. Every mortgage product between conventional loans and niche alternatives carries its own set of benefits and limitations, along with distinct qualifying rules. Your financial planning becomes more targeted when you understand the differences between various loan types. From conventional loans to niche alternatives, each product carries unique advantages, drawbacks, and qualification criteria. You can tailor your financial approach to your specific investment goals by learning how these loans differ.

Conventional Mortgages:

Conventional loans typically require stronger credit profiles and larger down payments often between 3% and 20% on owner-occupied transactions. They come in both fixed-rate and adjustable-rate forms. Investors who want long-term financial consistency benefit from fixed-rate mortgages because they provide unchanging monthly payments and cost predictability during the entire loan term. An adjustable-rate mortgage (ARM) provides an initial lower rate, which changes after a predetermined duration. An adjustable-rate mortgage reduces upfront costs and liberates funds for property improvements or new acquisitions but exposes you to potential payment increases as interest rates change. Investors who want to sell properties quickly or refinance before interest rates change might find an ARM to be their best option when market conditions remain supportive. However, when it comes to an ARM, it is always a good idea to be aware of the cap rate. In an adjustable-rate mortgage (ARM), your interest rate can change after an initial fixed period. For example, suppose you take out a 3/1 ARM at a 3% interest rate.

• First three years (the "3" in 3/1): Your interest rate is fixed at 3%. Your monthly payments remain consistent throughout this initial period, making budgeting easier.

• Subsequent years (the "1" in 3/1): At the end of the three-year fixed term, the loan's interest rate can adjust up or down once a year by no more than 1% based on a predetermined financial index (such as the U.S. Treasury rate or the LIBOR). If market rates rise significantly, you may see your interest rate rise in this example by 1%, and thus your monthly payment increase. Conversely, you might benefit from lower monthly costs if overall rates drop.

For instance, let's say that after your first three years, at 3%, market rates climb, and your new interest rate becomes 4%. As a result of the rate increase, your monthly mortgage payment will undoubtedly go up in the fourth year to reflect the higher rate. This added variability is why ARMs can be advantageous for those investors who plan to sell or refinance before the adjustment period starts because they can secure a lower initial rate yet pose a risk if rates surge and you remain in the property long-term.

Short Scenario Example (ARM):

Consider an investor who plans to complete a property flip within a two-year timeframe. He chose a 3/1 ARM, which ensures a low fixed rate for an initial three-year period. He uses this time to market and upgrade the property because low monthly payments allow him to invest more in renovations. He will be able to maximize profit on his flipped property while avoiding future interest rate increases by selling before the rate adjustment. Despite their inherent risk, ARMs demonstrate effectiveness in short-term transactions through the strategic planning of timelines and exit strategies.

FHA Loans:

FHA loans present a pragmatic alternative for first-time buyers or those with limited capital. Backed by the Federal Housing Administration (FHA), these mortgages allow lower down payments (as little as 3.5%) and are more tolerant when it comes to credit scores (FHA PowerSaver loans – CleanTechies). By easing typical qualification hurdles, FHA loans enable newcomers to join the real estate market without needing substantial upfront cash. With FHA loans, borrowers are required to pay mortgage insurance premiums (MIP), which increase their total monthly payments. It is because of PMI (Private Mortgage Insurance & MIP Mortgage Insurance Premiums) that banks can provide mortgage products with low down payments. Before the institution of these mortgage insurance products, the minimum downpayment was usually 20%. The benefits of instant home ownership and incremental equity growth make this exchange valuable for numerous buyers. Remember, FHA loans are commonly known as "owner-occupied loans." These loans serve mainly to finance homes that borrowers plan to live in as their primary residence.

VA Loans:

The Department of Veterans Affairs provides a potent financing option through VA loans, which service members, veterans, and particular eligible spouses can use. These loans attract service members transitioning to civilian life because they typically need no down payment and provide beneficial terms. Reduced interest rates, minimal closing costs, and flexible credit requirements all serve to support long-term wealth creation. VA loans can significantly reduce initial financial barriers for veterans launching new ventures or expanding existing portfolios. Again, please note that, like FHA loans, VA loans are considered owner-occupied loans.

Non-QM (Non-Qualified Mortgage) Loans:

This is a type of mortgage that many people don't know about. Non-QM (non-qualified mortgage) loans cater to borrowers whose financial profiles do not fit neatly into the traditional "qualified mortgage" (QM) requirements set by regulatory bodies such as the Consumer Financial Protection Bureau (CFPB). QM loans are structured to safeguard lenders and borrowers through strict debt-to-income (DTI) ratios and employment verification standards. Still, non-QM loans provide more adaptable assessment methods for borrower qualification. Non-QM loans serve as a valuable financing solution, especially for self-employed individuals, real estate investors, retirees, foreign nationals, and people with complicated income patterns who face difficulties conforming to traditional mortgage documentation and credit standards.

Let's take a look at David, who has worked as a self-employed marketing consultant for over five years and generated substantial income through several client contracts. Traditional lenders presented obstacles when he decided to buy a house despite his financial achievements. Banks classified him as a high-risk borrower since his monthly income varied, and he lacked a traditional W-2 paycheck. The deductions on his tax returns created an illusion of him earning significantly less than his actual income. The strict DTI ratio requirements and the employment verification standards (minimum of two years of continuous employment) of conventional mortgage programs hindered David's ability to secure a loan.

David pursued non-QM loan options as a potential financing option because these loans serve borrowers whose incomes are complex. Through his collaboration with a loan specialist, David was able to qualify for his loan by presenting two years of his business bank statements. This method was used to determine his actual income by calculating the amount of deposits from the past two years instead of using tax return verification. The lender reviewed his business revenue data alongside assets and expenses to determine his financial stability despite his income variations. The non-QM loan offered him more flexible options to evaluate his financial background compared to traditional mortgages.

The alternative financing solution enabled David to obtain a mortgage with favorable conditions that allowed him to buy his desired home without changing his business structure or tax approach. Non-QM loans offered him enough flexibility to overcome usual lending obstacles and achieve homeownership according to his personal preferences. Through this financing option, David demonstrated that self-employed individuals can obtain mortgages without meeting strict lending guidelines, which allowed him to convert his business achievements into property ownership.

Flexibility in Income Verification:

One of the most significant advantages of non-QM loans is that their lenders accept different income verification types, which enables borrowers with fluctuating or seasonal incomes to secure approval more readily (MULTI HOME LOANS LLC). Non-QM lenders can use different verification methods, while traditional mortgage lenders primarily depend on pay stubs and tax documents (MULTI HOME LOANS LLC). A willingness to consider alternative forms of income verification allows borrowers with variable, seasonal, or commission-based earnings to qualify more easily. Unlike traditional mortgage lenders that rely heavily on pay stubs, W-2s, and tax returns, non-QM lenders may accept:

• Bank statement loans, where borrowers demonstrate income consistency through 12 to 24 months of bank deposits rather than tax documents.

• High-worth individuals can qualify for asset-based loans by providing substantial liquid assets instead of traditional income streams.

• Debt-service coverage ratio (DSCR) loans cater to real estate investors by allowing them to qualify based on a property's rental income rather than their personal income.

For instance, a self-employed entrepreneur who reinvests business revenue for tax efficiency may have difficulty demonstrating sufficient taxable income to meet QM loan requirements. Through consistent bank statement deposits, non-QM bank statement loans enable borrowers to qualify and pursue homeownership or investments even if their tax returns show a low adjusted gross income.

Accommodating Unique Credit Situations:

Non-QM loans provide financial solutions for people who have experienced credit difficulties yet remain eligible for credit. Most traditional lenders reject borrowers who have filed for bankruptcy or had foreclosure incidents or late payments and mandate that they wait several years before they can regain loan eligibility. In contrast, non-QM lenders may offer:

• Shorter seasoning periods for bankruptcies and foreclosures, enabling borrowers to secure financing sooner.

• Higher DTI ratio allowances benefit individuals with significant assets or investment potential but high monthly obligations. What is DTI, you ask? Simply put, DTI is the amount of your monthly income needed to pay your monthly expenses. For instance, if your monthly expenses (mortgage + other credit obligations) equals $5000 a month and your income is $10,000, then your DTI is 50. In other words, it takes 50% of your monthly income to pay your total monthly expenses.

• Interest-only payment options that provide lower monthly costs during the loan's early years, which is advantageous for investors looking to maximize cash flow.

For example, an investor recovering from a recent foreclosure may find it nearly impossible to obtain a traditional loan due to the strict post-foreclosure waiting period imposed by most lenders. However, a non-QM portfolio lender may consider the investor's current financial stability, rental income streams, and overall investment strategy, allowing them to re-enter the market more quickly.

Higher Interest Rates and Risk Considerations:

Because non-QM loans serve borrowers who fall outside standard underwriting guidelines, they generally come with higher interest rates and more significant down payment requirements to offset the lender's increased risk. These rates vary based on creditworthiness, loan type, and market conditions, but they tend to be 1-3% higher than conventional mortgage rates. In addition, non-QM loans may include:

• Prepayment penalties, which discourage early refinancing into a lower-rate loan.

• Shorter loan terms, often with adjustable-rate structures instead of 30-year fixed-rate options.

• Higher origination fees, as lenders take on additional risk.

Despite these higher costs, real estate investors and strategic borrowers often use non-QM loans as a short-term financing solution to acquire properties quickly, generate rental income, and later refinance into a more favorable loan when their financial profile improves. Also, remember this. Real Estate is one of the few investments in which your tenants pay back the debt on your properties. So, despite the higher interest rate, if you calculate your rental income correctly, you should be able to offset the slightly higher interest rate.

Expanding Investment Opportunities with Non-QM Loans:

For real estate investors, non-QM loans are particularly valuable in a competitive market as they allow for faster approvals and fewer income-related hurdles. Many fix-and-flip investors, short-term rental hosts, and commercial real estate buyers use non-QM products to acquire properties that traditional lenders might reject due to property conditions or borrower complexity.

For example:

• The debt-service coverage ratio (DSCR) of a multi-family rental property enables investors to qualify for purchase instead of relying solely on their personal income, which leads to improved leverage and portfolio expansion opportunities.

• A house flipper seeking to buy, renovate, and sell a property quickly may use a non-QM bridge loan to secure fast funding, complete renovations, and refinance or sell within a short time frame.

• A foreign national looking to invest in U.S. real estate may lack a U.S. credit score but still qualify through foreign asset verification and bank statements, enabling them to expand their portfolio internationally.

Non-QM loans provide flexible, alternative financing solutions. By accommodating self-employed individuals, real estate investors, and those with unique financial circumstances, these loans expand access to homeownership and investment opportunities. While they typically come with higher interest rates and additional fees, the benefits including alternative income verification, faster approval times, and the ability to leverage rental income for qualification make them an attractive option for creative dealmakers. When used strategically, non-QM loans empower borrowers to bypass the rigid constraints of conventional financing and take advantage of lucrative opportunities in the real estate market (Built for Real Estate).

Securing a Mortgage:

Understanding how to secure a mortgage goes beyond filling out application forms. It requires intentional preparation, careful lender selection, and knowledge of key terms to increase your chances of obtaining favorable financing. When a bank is considering you for qualification, they are looking to answer four questions in order to approve you.

No. 1 – Are you able to pay the loan back? This is demonstrated in your pay stub. Do you make enough income?

No. 2: Can you afford to buy the property? This is demonstrated in your bank statements. Do you have the necessary assets on hand to cover your down payment and closing costs?

No. 3 – What is your willingness to pay back the loan? This is demonstrated through your credit report. The higher your score, the more willingness indicated.

No. 4 – Is the property worth what you are paying for, and is the title clean? This is why the banks always insist on an appraisal and title search as part of the mortgage process.

When it comes to processing the loan, all of the paperwork and questions regarding the processing of the loan are centered around those four questions.

Organizing Financial Documents:

Traditional lenders determine your creditworthiness by analyzing pay stubs, bank statements, tax returns, and existing debt records (Webber, 2022). Your application process may face delays because of inconsistent information or missing paperwork. Reviewing your credit report and resolving any inaccuracies before applying will help you prepare for a smooth application process. The presentation of a clean financial package proves your dependability and builds trust with lenders about your borrowing capability.

Not all lenders offer the same rates or fee structures. Comparing at least three institutions ranging from national banks to local credit unions can help you find the best match. While conventional lenders may focus on credit scores and down payments, more specialized lenders might cater to veterans or first-time buyers (e.g., VA or FHA loans). Evaluating each lender's unique terms against your own needs ensures you secure a loan arrangement that supports both short-term affordability and long-term growth. Back in my mortgage broker days, I discovered that different banks seem to be suitable for certain loans. For instance, some of my FHA lenders were not that good at processing conventional loans and vice versa when it came to some of my conventional lenders processing an FHA or VA loan.

The Pre-approval is a more rigorous process than a simple pre-qualification. A pre-approval involves carefully reviewing your submitted income, debt, and asset documentation. Whereas with a pre-qualification, a bank will take your initial word that you qualify for the mortgage based on the stated income and credit score you convey. However, once you find a property and are ready to put in an offer, you will be required to submit the necessary documents to prove the verbal information you provided was correct. Once approved for a certain amount, you gain clarity on your budget and demonstrate to sellers that you're a serious candidate. This positioning can expedite the process of creating a deal, particularly in competitive markets, since you've already shown an ability to fulfill your financial obligations (The Mortgage Loan Process in 9 Steps | Pre-Approval to Closing, 2020).

Key Loan Terms to Understand

• APR (Annual Percentage Rate):

• The Annual Percentage Rate (APR) demonstrates the complete yearly expense of borrowing, which includes both the declared interest rate and all loan-associated fees and additional costs. APR delivers a full assessment of borrowing costs, including origination fees, discount points, closing costs, and other lender-imposed charges in addition to the principal amount's interest rate. APR assists borrowers in comparing loan offers more precisely because loans with the same interest rate can have different APRs due to varying fees. APR standardizes borrowing expenses, improving lending transparency and letting borrowers understand their actual financing costs over time. The APR fails to reflect variable costs like prepayment penalties or changing interest rates in adjustable-rate mortgages, so borrowers must scrutinize loan terms to understand their complete financial responsibility.

• **Fixed vs. Adjustable Rate:**

The decision to choose between a fixed-rate mortgage vs an adjustable-rate mortgage (ARM) will significantly impact the stability and predictability of monthly payments over the life of the loan (Brickwood Mortgage). As mentioned before, a fixed-rate mortgage will retain the same interest rate for the entire term of the loan, thereby ensuring consistent monthly payments, which makes budgeting a lot easier while at the same time protecting borrowers from market fluctuations. This option is ideal for long-term stability and predictability in housing expenses. In contrast, an adjustable-rate mortgage features an interest rate that periodically changes based on market conditions, typically after an initial fixed period. And again, while ARMs usually start with lower interest rates than fixed-rate mortgages which makes them attractive to borrowers looking for lower initial payments they also carry the risk of rate increases over time, potentially leading to higher monthly payments (Churchill Mortgage).

The variability of an ARM can be beneficial if interest rates decrease or the borrower intends to sell or refinance before the rate has had a chance to adjust. However, a fixed-rate mortgage is usually the more safer choice for those who want financial certainty and protection against rising interest rates (What's the difference between fixed-rate and adjustable-rate mortgages in Oregon?). Understanding the differences between these two loan structures is very important in determining which option aligns best with an individual's financial goals and risk tolerance.

• Mortgage Insurance: Required in some instances (like FHA loans) to protect the lender in the event of default. When it comes to conventional loans, any down payment of less than 20% will require Private Mortgage Insurance (PMI) (New FHA Changes). With a conventional mortgage, you can drop the PMI when you prove that you have more than 20% equity in your property. This is usually done by the owner, who has an appraisal conducted on the property. On the other hand, with an FHA mortgage, you cannot drop the MIP even when your equity exceeds 20%. To get rid of MIP from an FHA loan, you will have to refinance it to a different mortgage.

• PITI Payment: When it comes to mortgage payments. The full monthly payments are broken down into four parts. Principal, Interest, Taxes (property taxes), and Insurance (homeowners' insurance). Thus, the term PITI payment. When getting a monthly payment quote from your bank, be sure to get the PITI payment quote, not just a quote for the principal and interest payment, which some loan officers love to give. Clarifying these points equips you to compare loan options thoroughly and avoid hidden costs or terms that might erode your profitability.

Impact of Interest Rates and Alternative Mortgage Solutions:

Your investment choices are significantly affected by current interest rate conditions. Investors benefit from low rates because they can secure cheaper loans, which enhance cash flow or allow for more significant acquisitions. When interest rates increase, they reduce investment potential through elevated monthly costs and reduced profit margins. Adapting your strategy to shifts in interest rates is key to sustaining long-term success in real estate.

Seller Financing:

Selling financing can be a welcome solution when a buyer struggles to qualify for a conventional loan or when the property in question doesn't meet standard loan requirements. Under this arrangement, the seller acts as the lender, allowing the buyer to pay them directly (Owner Financing). Flexible terms allow for better adjustment to distinctive financial scenarios compared to strict institutional guidelines. Seller financing usually reduces approval duration and decreases closing costs but often entails higher interest rates or requires balloon payments (a large principal payment due at the end of the loan term). Both parties should draft clear, legally sound contracts to avoid disputes down the road.

Hard Money Loans:

Hard money loans provide swift access to capital for projects needing rapid turnaround such as property flips or substantial renovations. Private investors offer these loans instead of traditional banks, and they come with higher interest rates but faster and simpler approval procedures. The property serves as collateral for these loans, which becomes attractive when a quick sale can mitigate higher borrowing expenses. To succeed with hard money financing, investors must plan exit strategies diligently, ensuring they don't carry the high-interest loan longer than necessary.

Real estate professionals needing immediate funding for property flipping or major renovations use hard money loans to gain swift access to capital. Private investors or lending groups fund hard money loans instead of traditional banks to enable faster and simpler approval processes. Borrowers benefit from early access to lucrative investment prospects that traditional banking procedures would have delayed.

The benefits of speed and convenience in hard money loans introduce specific trade-offs. The elevated interest rates on hard money loans mirror the increased risk and limited terms that characterize these types of financing. Borrowers commonly face substantial origination fees along with more demanding loan terms that feature shorter repayment periods, which typically span from six months to three years. To achieve profitability with these terms demands meticulous planning along with efficient execution.

Hard money loans operate based on a property-backed system where the financed asset itself acts as collateral. The lending practice focuses more on the potential market value of the asset than the borrower's credit history or financial condition. Investors who face limitations in traditional financing due to their financial backgrounds or credit scores find these loan terms especially beneficial.

Achieving success with hard money loans requires thorough and detailed strategic planning. Investors must establish definitive exit plans that usually involve selling the asset swiftly or transitioning to a long-term loan with reduced interest to avoid expensive loan payments. Investors must focus on managing renovation schedules precisely while conducting accurate market evaluations and implementing aggressive resale marketing tactics to keep their investments profitable despite increased borrowing expenses.

Real estate investors find hard money loans beneficial due to their flexibility and quick availability in competitive situations. However, they need disciplined planning and careful financial management to avoid high lending costs while maximizing benefits.

Staying Nimble with Changing Rates:

Market dynamics can shift quickly, so a flexible approach can yield significant advantages. For instance, if you lock in a fixed rate at historically low levels, you insulate yourself from future rate hikes an attractive prospect for long-term holds. A decline in rates will make shorter loan terms or adjustable-rate mortgages advantageous as they allow you to refinance under better conditions. Developing this adaptability will enable you to maintain your financial path through changing economic conditions.

Summary and Reflections:

In this chapter, we have delved into the many facets of mortgage selection and the practical steps involved in securing loan approval. From conventional loans fixed-rate and adjustable to government-backed products like FHA and VA loans to non-QM loans, each option presents its own advantages. Seller financing and hard money loans represent creative methods that can create new investment opportunities for those who choose paths beyond traditional banking. To secure advantageous mortgage conditions, buyers must fully organize their financial data, pick a lender who matches their objectives, and evaluate pre-approval options.

Understanding the impact of interest rate movements on profitability enables investors to maintain active control over their investment strategies. The combination of thorough preparation, strategic product choices, and adaptability to market changes allows real estate investors to use financing as a powerful growth lever. The mortgage paths presented in this guide enable both new investors and portfolio expanders to hasten their progress toward financial independence. Adopt these insights to refine your strategies to ensure that each decision yields short-term benefits and sustained future stability.

FHA Power Saver Loans – Clean Techies:

MultiHome Loans LLC.:

Investor Relationship Management Purpose – Built for Real Estate | Homebase:

Fixed vs. Adjustable-Rate Mortgages - Brickwood Mortgage:

Loan Programs | Churchill Mortgage:

What's the difference between fixed-rate and adjustable-rate mortgages in Oregon?

New FHA Changes – Again:

Owner Financing:

Ch. 4 - Mastering Cash Flow

Acquiring success in real estate investment requires competence in managing cash flow. Also needed is the ability to understand cash flow management, which enables investors to identify strategies that will boost earnings and fortify financial stability. Analyzing cash movement through each property provides the necessary insight to make well-informed choices ranging from finding valuable investments to recognizing possible risks. For both single-family home managers and apartment complex owners, cash flow awareness separates profitable long-term assets from burdensome financial challenges.

In this chapter, you will explore the methods used to assess and optimize cash flow, charting a path toward greater financial independence. We'll look at practical ways to compare rental income against operating expenses for a transparent view of your portfolio's performance. You'll also discover how debt service shapes your bottom line and why strategic financing can accelerate growth. Our discussion will address minimizing low vacancy rates and using cash flow statements to identify future opportunities. Integrating these factors will enable you to establish a powerful portfolio with lasting value that underpins your ongoing achievements in real estate.

Understanding Cash Flow in Real Estate:

Cash flow represents the net income from a property after all relevant expenses are accounted for (Why Accurate Cash Flow Projections...). This figure is crucial because it indicates how effectively your investment is performing and whether it can sustain ongoing operations or fund additional ventures. Positive cash flow demonstrates that a property earns sufficient income to pay expenses and make a profit, but negative cash flow indicates that expenses surpass revenue, which could create financial stress.

Several key factors influence cash flow:

Rental Income: Your primary revenue source is shaped by market demand, property location, and condition. Fluctuations in tenant preferences or local economic changes can alter rental income over time.

Operating Expenses: Recurring costs (e.g., insurance, property taxes, utilities, maintenance) are essential to the property's upkeep. Keeping these expenses in check directly affects profitability (Landon, n.d.).

Debt Service: Mortgage payments or any other loan obligations tied to the property. Ensuring your financing terms align with rental income helps maintain a stable balance between incoming and outgoing cash (Editor, 2022).

Vacancy Rates: Every month, a unit remains unoccupied, which represents lost income.

The cash flow statement integrates these components by categorizing income and expenses into operating, investing, and financing sections. The statement shows how your property business handles its monetary transactions. Frequent examination of cash flow statements reveals potential inefficiencies and improvement opportunities. Through standardized metrics such as Net Operating Income (NOI) and Debt Service Coverage Ratio (DSCR), you can maintain consistent comparisons between different properties (Maximizing Your ROI).

• Net Operating Income (NOI) demonstrates how profitable operations are before considering financing expenditures.

This real estate investment property example illustrates how to calculate Net Operating Income (NOI) in a straightforward manner. Scenario: A rental property generates income for its investor while also requiring operating expense payments.

Step-by-Step Calculation:

Gross Rental Income:
• Annual Rent Collected: $50,000

Operating Expenses (annual):
• Property Taxes: $5,000
• Insurance: $2,000
• Maintenance and Repairs: $3,000
• Property Management Fees: $4,000
• Utilities (owner-paid): $1,000
Total Operating Expenses: $5,000 + $2,000 + $3,000 + $4,000 + $1,000 = $15,000

Net Operating Income (NOI) Calculation:
Calculate Net Operating Income (NOI) by subtracting Operating Expenses from Gross

Rental Income.
Substituting the numbers:
NOI=$50,000–$15,000=$35,000

Final Result: • Net Operating Income (NOI) = $35,000 per year

Interpretation: NOI demonstrates the property's operational profitability each year, excluding mortgage payments and income tax expenses. Investors utilize Net Operating Income (NOI) to evaluate and compare potential real estate investment opportunities.

• The DSCR metric evaluates how well a property can manage its debt obligations through its Net Operating Income divided by total debt payments.

Here's a clear, straightforward example illustrating the Debt Service Coverage Ratio: Scenario:
• Net Operating Income (NOI): $35,000 per year.

Additional   Assumption:
• Annual Debt Service (mortgage payments): $25,000

The Debt Service Coverage Ratio is calculated as follows:

* Net Operating Income (NOI) – divided by - Annual Debt Service DSCR = DSCR

$35,000 (NOI) - divided by - $25,000 (Annual Debt Service = 1.40 DSCR

Final   Result:
• Debt Service Coverage Ratio (DSCR) = 1.40

Interpretation: A DSCR of 1.40 means the property generates 40% more income than needed to cover the annual debt payments, indicating good financial health. Typically, lenders prefer a DSCR of at least 1.25, signaling sufficient cash flow to manage debt comfortably.

These measures serve as anchors for strategic decisions. Used alongside the cash-on-cash return, the ratio of annual pre-tax cash flow to total cash invested helps you gauge the effectiveness of an investment relative to the actual dollars you've put in.

Key Takeaways:

• Positive cash flow hinges on balancing rental income with ongoing expenses and debt service.

• Reviewing your cash flow statements on a regular basis will help to pinpoint problem areas and opportunities for improvement (Basic and Advanced Cash Flow Strategies).

• Metrics like NOI, DSCR, and cash-on-cash return enable a consistent comparison of different investment properties.

Evaluating Rental Properties for Cash Flow Potential:

Potential investors must conduct thorough assessments of rental properties to confirm they will yield profitable cash flow before making any commitments. Understanding the market initiates a structured approach that proceeds to detail costs before establishing rent, followed by inspecting the property for possible problems.

Market Research: To evaluate local rental demand, it is important to examine relevant trends, including population expansion, employment opportunities, and infrastructure development.

The targeted area's demographic changes and lifestyle preferences present essential factors that define rental demand. As younger professionals move into an area, they tend to prefer rental properties with modern amenities alongside convenient public transit options and lively local cultural activities. Family-friendly neighborhoods focus their appeal on superior educational institutions along with secure parks and community spaces. By understanding these nuances, you can optimize your investment strategy and marketing campaigns, which leads to higher occupancy rates and greater tenant satisfaction.

By keeping track of upcoming developments, along with zoning modifications and business growth plans, we can detect trends that will affect the rental market. Real estate professionals who connect with local government offices and community organizations can discover important information about future developments that remain unknown to most people. Investors who actively monitor their local economic environment can find new opportunities while reducing risks to maintain superior market positioning against competitors who lack this information.

Detailed Expense Analysis: Mortgage payments, along with property taxes and insurance, should be classified as fixed expenses, while maintenance work and repairs need to be categorized as variable expenses. Distinguish between fixed expenses, such as mortgage payments and property taxes, and variable costs, including maintenance work and utility bills. Throughout the loan term, fixed costs stay stable, but variable costs change according to occupancy levels and seasonal conditions alongside unexpected issues. Allocating a specific reserve fund for unpredictable and variable expenses preserves steady cash flow and lowers financial exposure to protect property investment returns.

Analyzing historical operating data from similar properties helps increase the precision of your expense projections. Real estate associations and property management firms offer industry benchmarks or standardized expense ratios that function as valuable guidelines. Businesses can minimize cash-flow disruptions from underestimated expenses or market changes by refining budget projections and understanding regional labor cost variations and utility rate shifts that enable proactive financial planning adjustments.

Rent Pricing Strategies: Property managers conduct extensive market analyses to adjust rent prices to stay competitive without setting their property value too low. Property managers should base their rental pricing decisions on nearby construction projects as well as local infrastructure enhancements and forthcoming business investments since these elements can markedly affect rental property value perception. The use of technology to monitor rental price movements and competitor offers generates meaningful insights which support better pricing decisions.

Property managers have the capability to improve their pricing and service strategies continuously through tenant feedback. Direct interaction with tenants to gather insights about their value perceptions plus expectations and satisfaction levels uncovers ways to boost perceived property value without cutting rent prices. Property managers can implement strategic upgrades to amenities alongside property enhancements and improved customer service to establish premium rent rates while building stronger tenant relationships over time.

In competitive markets, property managers utilize revenue management software alongside predictive analytics to establish rental prices with strategic precision. These tools enable property managers to establish optimal pricing through analysis of past data trends combined with competitor market positioning and future market development forecasts for better decision-making. Through the use of these insights, property managers can predict renter demand patterns in advance and establish rental prices that ensure financial success while remaining appealing to potential tenants.

Diversifying lease structures proves advantageous for sustaining consistent occupancy rates while securing steady cash flow. Flexible lease arrangements like premium short-term rentals and discounted long-term leases respond to diverse tenant requirements while expanding potential renter demographics. Through flexible property management tactics, owners can draw diverse tenant groups while maintaining steady rental revenues and minimizing the threat of extended vacant periods.

Property Inspections: Physically walking through the building reveals wear and tear that might not appear in financial statements. Look closely at the state of major systems like plumbing, electrical wiring, and HVAC to estimate repair costs (How to Conduct an Accurate Rental Property Cash Flow Analysis, 2024). Early detection of these needs enables purchase price negotiations or directs future upgrade budget plans.

Professional property assessments provide additional accuracy to visual inspections for the detection of possible hidden issues and liabilities. A certified inspector provides impartial assessments of structural soundness and safety while verifying code adherence. Professional inspections frequently uncover hidden problems such as foundational damage, concealed water damage, mold infestations, or out-of-date electrical systems, which could lead to substantial unexpected repair costs if ignored. Detailed assessments generate negotiation advantages and guide sound investment choices.

Property inspections serve as essential tools for devising strategic property enhancements that boost both value and marketability. Thorough inspection data allows property owners to determine essential upgrade priorities and preventive maintenance actions that prevent major system breakdowns while making the property more attractive to potential renters. Physical inspections lead to informed maintenance planning, which helps extend the life of the building components while cutting operational expenses and boosting profitability.

Key Takeaways:

• Market analysis enables realistic rent calculations and competitive rate setting.

• Complete reviews of all expenses, including fixed and variable costs, to prevent cost underestimation.

• Physical inspections help you gauge maintenance expenses and strengthen your negotiating position.

Enhancing Cash Flow Strategies:

Selecting the right property marks only the start of the process. Operational management alongside incremental improvements drives substantial cash flow growth over time.

Regularly adjusting the rent to reflect market conditions can boost income without alienating reliable tenants (12 Ways to Increase Rental Property Cash Flow | Mynd Management, 2022).

Transparency and advanced notice about rent increases fosters trust and reduce tenant turnover. Keep local regulations in mind when determining rent-raise limits or timelines.

Strategic cost-cutting measures can have an immediate impact on net cash flow. Negotiating better rates with service providers or upgrading to energy-efficient appliances are two proven tactics (How to Increase Cash Flow from a Rental Property, 2024). While improvements might incur upfront expenses, they often pay for themselves through lower monthly bills and stronger tenant demand.

Effective property marketing and tenant screening processes contribute significantly to improved cash flow management. Targeted advertising channels help attract qualified prospective renters, which leads to shorter vacancy periods and more stable rental income. Property owners benefit from thorough tenant screenings that include background checks and credit assessments because they result in reliable tenants who pay rent punctually and take care of the property, therefore minimizing both maintenance costs and tenant turnover expenses.

Financial success over the long term depends greatly on keeping open professional communication channels with tenants. By immediately responding to tenant concerns and maintenance requests, property managers improve tenant satisfaction, which in turn motivates tenants to renew leases, thus maintaining stable occupancy rates. Streamlined management software enables efficient control over tenant communications and payments as well as maintenance problem tracking, which results in better operational flow and improved tenant-landlord connections.

Renovations with High ROI:

Target renovations that improve rental value focus on key areas such as kitchens and bathrooms. An excellent renovation enables landlords to charge higher rent while drawing dependable tenants. Scheduling renovations during planned vacancies (e.g., between leases) reduces disruption and ensures continued cash flow from other units (12 Ways to Increase Rental Property Cash Flow | Mynd Management, 2022).

Updating essential components of a rental property apart from kitchen and bathroom improvements can greatly boost its attractiveness to potential renters. Tech-savvy tenants find properties with energy-efficient appliances and smart home technologies like smart locks and thermostats more appealing, which allows landlords to charge premium rental prices. Investing in curb appeal through fresh exterior paint jobs alongside improved landscaping and entryway maintenance delivers strong first impressions, which boosts demand and shortens vacancy periods. Strategic renovations boost both property appearance and functionality, which leads to property value growth that helps landlords achieve higher investment returns.

Transforming underused spaces into usable living areas represents a high-ROI renovation strategy. Landlords can turn basements into extra rental units while unused dining areas can become home offices, along with space optimization through improved storage solutions. These property improvements meet the evolving demands of tenants who now prioritize space efficiency in densely populated urban locations. Landlords who provide in-unit laundry facilities together with upgraded HVAC systems for energy efficiency and durable, low-maintenance materials will experience reduced maintenance expenses and attract long-term renters who appreciate convenience and comfort. Strategic high-impact renovations enable landlords to increase rents and tenant retention, which will boost property value while securing a strong investment return over time.

Tenant Management:

Property managers serve as essential figures in ensuring tenants experience a positive living environment. Thorough tenant screening stands out as one of the most efficient methods to achieve positive tenant relations and property management goals. Tenant screening means property managers evaluate prospective renters to determine their suitability for the property. The screening process for tenants usually encompasses background checks along with credit history assessments and reference checks from past landlords. Proper tenant screening enables property managers to minimize problems that could emerge throughout the lease period.

A property manager gets a prospective tenant application. The applicant appeared pleasant during their meeting, yet their credit history indicates several late payments. The property manager may decide to seek a tenant with better financial stability instead of approving this current application. This choice protects the property while guaranteeing that incoming tenants have the financial ability to maintain their rental payments.

Communication:

Property managers must maintain open communication channels to build positive relationships with tenants along with conducting thorough screening. Good communication involves being approachable and responsive. Property managers need to develop a welcoming atmosphere that allows tenants to comfortably bring forward their questions and concerns. A variety of communication methods, including phone calls, email messages, and text messaging systems, should be available for tenants to contact property management.

Tenants who receive quick replies to their concerns will feel appreciated and treated with respect. A property manager who responds quickly to tenant inquiries about lease agreements or property rules helps avoid tenant frustration. Regular communication through emails and community events strengthens tenant connections with the property management team.

Maintenance Requests:

Responding quickly to maintenance requests helps build tenant loyalty. Quick attention to maintenance concerns lets tenants know that their comfort and safety take precedence. When property managers address a reported leaking faucet quickly it substantially improves the tenant's living conditions. When property managers arrange repairs without delay, they show tenants their dependability and attentiveness.

Property managers can establish an efficient maintenance response system through the creation of an accessible maintenance request platform. An online platform for tenants to submit maintenance requests allows them to detail the severity of the issue and attach photos when necessary. Property managers who streamline their request process can maintain effective tracking of service requests and achieve prompt resolution of issues. Regular follow-up practices help tenants feel supported throughout their stay at the property.

Lease Agreements:

Successful property management depends on lease agreements that are both clear and detailed. A properly written lease needs to present the rental agreement terms and conditions in a transparent manner. The lease agreement needs to detail rent payment schedules and security deposits as well as explain tenant responsibilities and shared space rules.

Understanding their obligations and expectations helps tenants prevent misunderstandings. The lease agreement specifies that tenants must pay rent on the first of each month, but they have five extra days to meet this obligation, which makes the tenant's responsibilities clear. Defining lease terms with clarity enables property managers to prevent future disputes.

Property managers must verify that lease agreements utilize simple language for clarity. Tenants have a better chance of understanding their rights and responsibilities when the lease agreement avoids complex legal jargon. Tenants who understand their lease terms tend to raise fewer disputes, which results in a smoother rental experience.

Building Tenant Loyalty:

When property managers use thorough tenant screening combined with open communication and quick maintenance responses along with clear lease agreements they achieve tenant loyalty. Tenants who perceive their rental situation as safe and appreciated demonstrate higher lease renewal rates. Property owners benefit from reduced turnover rates and lower costs to find new tenants because tenant loyalty results in longer-term leases.

Tenants who witness their property manager responding to their feedback promptly typically develop greater satisfaction with their rental experience. Tenants who feel content with their living situation demonstrate their happiness through lease renewal. Property managers benefit from stable rental income because they don't have to worry about filling vacant units frequently.

Property managers who prioritize tenant needs can generate a comfortable living atmosphere for residents. The resulting tenant satisfaction can become positive word-of-mouth referrals, which further strengthen the property manager's community reputation.

Conclusion of Principles:

Property managers must recognize their significant role in developing tenant satisfaction through positive interactions. Through solid tenant screening processes and clear lease agreements combined with quick maintenance responses and open communication channels, property managers establish strong tenant loyalty foundations. Successful property management relies heavily on maintaining tenant satisfaction.

It is essential to establish a living space where tenants experience respect and value. By implementing these strategies, property managers can achieve improved tenant satisfaction and create a flourishing rental community.

Key Takeaways:

• Periodic, moderate rent increases can align revenue with market rates.

• Whether through vendor negotiations or energy-efficient upgrades, cost reductions favorably impact net cash flow.

• Thoughtful renovations attract quality tenants and justify higher rents, while proactive tenant management minimizes turnover.

Summary and Reflections

For real estate portfolios to maintain profitability while expanding their holdings, mastery over cash flow remains essential. Evaluating property performance requires you to understand multiple factors, including rental income and operating expenses, together with debt service and vacancy rates. The use of essential metrics such as NOI, DSCR, and cash-on-cash return gives you greater confidence when evaluating potential opportunities while enabling effective tracking of asset performance.

Solid market research, coupled with realistic expense evaluations and thorough property inspections, establishes a reliable basis for making prudent investment decisions. Targeted strategies, including gradual rent increases along with cost containment, selective renovations, and strong tenant management, can drive upward cash flow after you purchase a property. By maintaining comprehensive records and consistently analyzing cash flow statements, you can detect early trends, allowing you to quickly respond to economic shifts.

Your real estate investments achieve lasting financial success through the adoption of these strategies. Through this chapter's guidance, you'll learn to unlock maximum financial value from every asset to build a robust, thriving portfolio. As you refine your approach to cash flow, every decision becomes an opportunity to strengthen your bottom line, secure better financing, and pave the way to a future of expanded possibilities in real estate investing.

References:

•Why Accurate Cash Flow Projections Are Essential for Real Estate Success. https://www.luminareia.com/post/why-accurate-cash-flow-projections-are-essential-for-real-estate-success

Maximizing Your ROI: Investment Strategies for Real Estate Success - korerealty.ca. https://korerealty.ca/maximizing-your-roi-investment-strategies-for-real-estate-success/

Basic and Advanced Cash Flow Strategies for SMEs - From Surviving to Thriving. https://genzed.co.uk/blog/basic-and-advanced-cash-flow-strategies-for-smes-from-surviving-to-thriving/

Editor. (2022). Mortgages and Debt Service in Real Estate. Property Financing Journal.

How to Conduct a Market Analysis for Your Rental Property | Blog | RentersWarehouse.com. (n.d.)

How to Increase Cash Flow from a Rental Property. (2024). Investment Property Insights.

Landon. (n.d.). Fundamentals of Operating Expenses. Landon Real Estate Press.

12 Ways to Increase Rental Property Cash Flow | Mynd Management. (2022).

Ch. 5 - Lease Options and Their Advantages

Savvy real estate investors can achieve investment flexibility through lease options while avoiding substantial initial capital expenditure. Investors find lease options to be a strategic choice within the real estate industry, which typically demands substantial financial investments because these options enable property examination and purchase with minimal starting capital. This chapter examines the fundamental principles of lease options and explains their appeal to present-day investors who aim to build adaptable portfolios. Lease options represent an active real estate investment strategy appropriate for current market conditions that attract investors who are looking for growth opportunities and financial stability.

The upcoming parts of this chapter will give a complete explanation of every element that distinguishes lease options. You can identify how lease options differ from standard rental contracts by examining core components such as contract length, rent payments, purchase costs, and option fees. Real-world examples demonstrate lease option benefits that enable a transition from renting to owning a home. The training teaches you to identify market situations where lease options reach their peak performance. The detailed research indicates that lease options are flexible instruments that support financial planning while providing insights into real estate investment decisions.

Defining Lease Options and Their Components:

Investors find that lease options stand out in investment strategies because they reduce initial capital needs while providing paths toward property ownership. A lease option represents a legal contract that provides a tenant the ability to buy the property at a predetermined point in time without being required to do so. Prospective homeowners and real estate investors obtain substantial benefits in uncertain markets by using this distinctive arrangement, which enables them to assess both properties and neighborhoods before committing to a purchase.

Duration:

The lease option agreement specifies the period during which buyers can choose to purchase the property. The duration of the agreement varies between several months to several years which acts as an extended "trial period." The length of time works as a critical component of success for investors who must stabilize their finances and improve their credit rating while also monitoring market trends. Extended durations provide more substantial protection from market volatility, which enables tenant-buyers sufficient time to evaluate the property's appreciation potential and neighborhood stability while matching their long-term financial and personal goals.

Monthly Rent:

A lease option agreement typically involves higher monthly rent than standard rentals because part of the rent contributes to a future down payment. A lease-option arrangement lets tenants build equity over time because typical leases do not offer this benefit. Both tenants and property owners need clear information about the rent accumulation for potential purchases. Clear documentation of rent credit arrangements helps eliminate confusion and build trust between tenants and property owners, which strengthens the stability and predictability of the agreement.

Example: While Emily desires to own her own home, she currently cannot secure a traditional mortgage because she does not have enough money for the down payment or sufficient credit history. Emily signs a two-year lease option contract for a townhouse. The monthly rent Emily pays exceeds standard rates in her area, but she knows this extra amount helps build her down payment.

The lease option agreement allows Emily to build equity for her future down payment during the agreement period since this advantage does not exist in standard rental contracts. Emily and her landlord, Mr. Patel, both maintain explicit records that show the precise amount from her monthly rent that goes toward the down payment credit. Transparent practices minimize misunderstandings between parties while building foundational trust between them.

Emily's monthly rent payments give her reassurance because she knows what to expect from the clear and predictable terms. The transparent rental agreement allows Mr. Patel to recognize the stability that emerges from Emily's committed and responsible tenancy. Emily has gathered sufficient down payment credit by her lease's conclusion which enables her to comfortably complete the townhouse purchase and transition seamlessly from renting to owning.

Purchase Price:

Setting the purchase price from the beginning protects tenants from rising local property values; investors who want to earn appreciation but lack mortgage qualification benefit from the ability to lock in the purchase price. When property values decrease, the tenant can choose to leave the deal to avoid financial losses.

Example: Michael is a prospective homeowner aiming to purchase property in a neighborhood experiencing rapid growth and rising property values. Aware of his current inability to secure immediate mortgage approval, Michael negotiates a lease option agreement for a desirable condominium. From the beginning, he and the property owner, Ms. Johnson, set and documented a fixed purchase price.

As local property values continue to rise substantially over the next two years, Michael benefits significantly from having locked in his purchase price at a previously agreed-upon lower value. This foresight protects Michael from market inflation and positions him advantageously when he is ready to finalize the purchase. Ms. Johnson also benefits from Michael's responsible management of the condominium and the security of steady rental income.

However, if the local property market had unexpectedly declined during the agreement period, Michael would still have the strategic flexibility to opt out, avoiding significant financial loss from purchasing a depreciated asset. Thus, clearly establishing the purchase price early in the lease option contract provided Michael crucial protection against market volatility, enhancing both his investment strategy and financial planning.

Option Fee (Option Consideration):

Often ranging between 1% and 7% of the property's value, the option fee is a non-refundable payment granting the tenant exclusive rights to purchase within the lease term. From the seller's perspective, the option fee signals a tenant-buyer's genuine commitment to the property, helps reduce turnover and vacancy risk, and encourages more responsible property care (since the tenant often plans to own the home). It also provides immediate, non-refundable income and can justify a slightly higher purchase price or rent. The seller retains the fee when a tenant decides against buying and is free to relist the property or create a new agreement to mitigate market changes. Sellers obtain confirmation of the tenant's genuine interest through this mechanism. Tenants find value in this arrangement by making a calculated investment towards their future property ownership.

Example: The single-family property that Mr. Thompson owns has remained unsold for a longer period than expected. To minimize the financial burden of vacancy costs and prevent property deterioration, he chooses to implement a lease option arrangement. Mr. Thompson begins discussions with Sarah, who wants to buy a home but lacks the immediate qualifications needed for a standard mortgage.

Sarah pays the upfront option fee that amounts to 5% of the property's value. Mr. Thompson views the substantial non-refundable option fee as a definitive indication of Sarah's authentic dedication to securing the property. Mr. Thompson gains both cash flow and protection against short-term vacancy through the fee, which significantly reduces his financial risk.

During the lease period, Mr. Thompson observed Sarah's continuous property maintenance and improvements, which reflect an owner's pride and responsibility. Mr. Thompson keeps the option fee when Sarah chooses not to buy the property, which helps him cover any costs and challenges he faces when he needs to market the property again. Plus, the fact that Sara improved the property means the house has maintained or increased in value. Mr. Thompson gains the confidence to draft a new lease option agreement or put the property up for sale based on current market conditions. The option fee delivers multiple strategic benefits, which include generating upfront income while minimizing vacancy risks and demonstrating tenant commitment.

Comparison and Real-World Applications of Lease Options:

Tenants committed to finding permanent housing or expanding their investments will often find Lease Options more attractive. Tenants who hold the option to purchase their leased property will frequently maintain and improve the property as if they were its owners.

Bridging the Rent–Own Gap: As mentioned before, lease options effectively bridge the gap between renting and owning by allowing tenants to accumulate equity (if specified in the agreement) while simultaneously building credit during the lease term. This structure can be especially attractive when lending criteria or down payment funds stand as barriers to the buyer's immediate purchase.

Motivated Seller Scenarios: Sellers who want to prevent extended vacancy periods might agree to lease option arrangements. A fixed purchase price combined with an option fee collection lets sellers lower their risks while continuing to receive regular rental income. Buyers will then have the opportunity to arrange advantageous terms, which may include reduced initial payments or adaptable payment schedules.

Comparative Advantage:

Traditional Rentals: Provide occupancy but no ownership path. Tenants typically have less incentive to maintain or improve the property.

Lease Options: These offer a tangible route to ownership; tenants are more invested in upkeep, potentially boosting property value for future sale.

Practical Insight:

An investor can find promising real estate deals by targeting sellers who need to sell quickly because they haven't found a buyer yet. A lease option lets the investor establish a future share in property appreciation without making a large initial down payment. Property value appreciation over time provides both the investor-tenant and the seller advantages through their structured sales agreement.

With lease options, both parties must carefully navigate the legal framework to create a contract that benefits both sides fairly. (Master Budget-Friendly Real Estate Investing: A Comprehensive Guide - Royal Oxford Global Properties).

Reduced Upfront Costs:

Entering a lease option demands much less capital compared to buying a property outright. This approach releases capital resources that investors can use to expand into multiple properties or cover unforeseen financial needs. Prospective buyers working to build their credit can use this lease option structure to improve their credit scores, which will help them obtain better financing options in the future. Real Estate Department | mvslalgeria.org.

Lease option tenants who avoid securing a mortgage from the start can evaluate both the cash flow potential and the livability of a property. Suppose the property does not achieve the anticipated performance from market shifts, neighborhood changes, or personal circumstances. In that case, buyers have the choice to walk away without facing mortgage sale consequences or foreclosure.

Legal Consideration - Regional Laws:

The legal interpretation and requirements for lease option agreements differ according to jurisdictional variations. In some regions, lease options function as rental agreements with extra conditions, but other regions treat them as purchase contracts with distinct legal obligations. Jurisdictional laws establish mandatory disclosures along with tenant rights related to option payments and enforceability limits for specific lease option terms. Researching thoroughly and seeking advice from regional housing authorities unveils critical legal details which help prevent contract disputes and invalidations.

Clear Contract Terms:

The lease option agreement effectively prevents misunderstandings and disputes by specifying obligations about insurance coverage and property taxes as well as possible homeowner association fees. A clear explanation of how tenant-installed improvements will affect property value at purchase time avoids future misunderstandings. Creating clear termination provisions and remedies for breach or non-performance protects both parties' interests and enables a more efficient contractual experience for everyone involved.

Professional Guidance:

Professionals with knowledge of lease options help organizations maintain regulatory compliance while gaining strategic benefits during contract negotiations. With professional assistance, parties can discover hidden risks or opportunities, like rent credit tax consequences, and receive guidance on forming agreements that achieve financial targets for both sides. Employing the knowledge of real estate attorneys and financial specialists enhances credibility and transparency in the process, which builds trust between parties and encourages collaboration to minimize expensive legal disagreements.

Key Reminders:

• Perform due diligence before signing by conducting a thorough property inspection and market research.

• Document precisely how rent premiums and option fees will be allocated toward the final purchase.

• To prevent legal deadlock situations, include clauses that allow for adjustments when market values fluctuate or personal financial situations change.

Summary and Reflections:

Lease options have emerged as a compelling real estate strategy, blending the flexibility of renting with the future potential of homeownership. Unlike traditional property investments that require substantial initial capital, lease options significantly reduce upfront financial barriers. Investors and prospective homeowners alike find this approach appealing, as it allows them to evaluate properties, neighborhoods, and market conditions thoroughly without immediate commitment. During the lease term, tenants pay higher monthly rents, part of which accumulates as equity, providing a strategic and incremental pathway toward ownership.

Several critical components define lease option agreements, including contract duration, monthly rent payments, purchase price determination, and the option fee. Lease periods vary from months to multiple years, offering tenants a valuable extended timeframe to build credit and financial stability while monitoring property appreciation. Setting a predetermined purchase price safeguards buyers from market fluctuations, providing protection if values rise and flexibility to withdraw if values fall. An upfront option fee, typically non-refundable, signals genuine buyer commitment and reduces seller risks associated with property vacancies or turnover.

Practical examples illustrate the real-world effectiveness of lease options. Individuals like Emily benefit directly by allocating part of their monthly rent towards future homeownership, enabling a seamless transition from renting to purchasing. Michael strategically secures a favorable purchase price ahead of anticipated property value increases, positioning himself advantageously despite current mortgage approval constraints. These scenarios demonstrate the broader value of lease options, offering both parties clarity, financial predictability, and mutual trust that typically enhances property care and maintenance.

Ultimately, successful lease option arrangements depend upon clearly defined contracts and careful financial planning. Transparent documentation of terms such as duration, monthly rent credits, and purchase conditions prevents misunderstandings and legal disputes. By enabling property ownership with reduced financial risk and providing stable rental income for property owners, lease options have become a favored strategy in contemporary real estate investing.

They empower individuals and investors to strategically enter the real estate market, thoughtfully manage risk, and progressively build equity and long-term wealth.

Checklist for Lease Option Success

• Confirm that the duration provides adequate time to secure financing or assess the property.

• Ensure all parties clearly document and understand monthly rent premiums and option fees.

• Investigate local regulations and, if necessary, enlist professional advice to finalize the contract.

• Maintain open communication with the property's owner or tenant to address concerns early and prevent misunderstandings.

Ch. 6 - Tools for Investment Analysis

Successful real estate investment depends on having access to appropriate analytical tools. Different property types, together with various market conditions, create challenges when analyzing market trends and processing large data sets. Analysis tools designed for specific purposes enable users to understand intricate data sets and better assess potential investments. Beginners use these analytical aids to transform market data into actionable insights that help with making informed decisions.

This chapter introduces a suite of powerful tools every real estate investor should consider integrating into their workflow. Spreadsheet software enables extensive flexibility in organizing financial data. At the same time, investment calculators deliver fast access to metrics such as ROI and Cap Rate so you can dedicate time to strategic planning. We'll also explore how real estate apps grant real-time access to property listings and market conditions, ensuring you can respond decisively to opportunities as they arise. Our next focus will be on how dashboards, combined with Comparative Market Analysis (CMA), refine your view of the properties you aim to buy. Combining these tools with knowledge of ROI and Cap Rate calculations will enable you to develop a strong data-backed investment strategy that meets your financial objectives.

Essential Investment Analysis Tools:

The decision-making process in real estate investing requires choosing and perfecting the proper instruments to transform haphazard decisions into precise strategies. These resources assist you in handling data while saving time when you evaluate cash flow for one deal or compare several properties.

Spreadsheet Software:

The industry consistently uses spreadsheets to organize property-related financial data, including acquisition costs, projected revenues, and future expense predictions. Designing custom templates enables users to analyze operating expenses through detailed breakdowns while modeling different scenarios and maintaining accurate monthly and annual cash flow records. For new investors, start with a simple template: list your expected income on one side and outflows (mortgage payments, repairs, insurance) on the other, and include a cell for your net operating income (NOI). As your portfolio expands, you can layer in more complex formulas like pro forma calculations for appreciation or rent increases without losing track of the bigger picture.

Spreadsheet software enables investors to conduct advanced investment comparisons beyond financial tracking by using charts and graphs to transform complex data into simple visuals for quick understanding. Through conditional formatting, investors can emphasize areas of concern by identifying when expenses surpass budgetary thresholds or when properties fail to meet revenue benchmarks and thus speed up their response time to these issues. Cloud-based spreadsheet software improves team or stakeholder cooperation by allowing simultaneous data editing along with real-time feedback and secure access from remote locations. Investors who master advanced spreadsheet features can optimize decision-making processes while boosting communication transparency and modifying strategies quickly to meet market changes.

Investment Calculators:

Quick, accurate calculations of core metrics (ROI, cash-on-cash return, debt service coverage) are essential for high-level deal evaluations. Online or app-based calculators can instantly parse your input data, such as purchase price, rental income, and financing details, to generate performance indicators. The speed at which you evaluate deals helps identify which ones require additional examination. Investment opportunity evaluations benefit from calculators because they provide rapid comparisons across numerous scenarios, although they fail to record every property detail.

Effective calculator use enables investors to integrate results with tools like Comparative Market Analyses (CMAs) and property inspections for a complete investment analysis. Investors can organize their performance tracking systems by embedding calculator results into spreadsheets or dashboards, which they can use to monitor current performance and compare it with historical data.

Investors achieve more precise strategies and anticipate risk while confirming their investment assumptions when they document calculated insights with qualitative market data. Integrated approaches enable investors to overcome the limitations of standalone calculators by delivering deeper financial understanding and improved investment precision.

Real Estate Apps:

Mobile technology has revolutionized how investors access market data. Real estate applications connect directly to Multiple Listing Services (MLS) or gather property information from users to deliver real-time updates on new listings as well as changes in prices and comparable sales data. Steady information updates and location-based features allow users to identify time-sensitive opportunities and ensure they don't miss out. You can quickly analyze local demographics and historical transaction records when you find an interesting property. Mortgage calculators and renovation cost estimators are now included in apps and are beneficial for new users because they accelerate initial budgeting and ROI estimation processes.

Modern real estate applications offer users the ability to maintain personalized property searches while also allowing them to set customized alerts and share listings with investment partners and real estate professionals. Investors can use advanced filtering tools to narrow down searches based on property type specifications, along with price range limitations, potential rental income figures, and neighborhood appeal. Mapping integrations reveal geographic trends together with property hotspots and new infrastructure projects that impact future property valuations. Investors who consistently use these advanced features gain better market insight and efficiently schedule viewings while getting ahead of the competition in active markets.

Dashboard Tools:

Dashboard tools provide transparent visualizations of your portfolio to those who manage multiple properties or seek detailed performance monitoring. These tools convert spreadsheets and raw data into visual representations that display occupancy rates, rental income patterns, and monthly expense details at a glance. Dashboards enable fast course corrections by highlighting patterns of a gradual dip in average rental rates or an unexpected spike in repair costs. If you work in a partnership or keep a property manager on staff, dashboards provide a shared snapshot of each asset's health, promoting collaborative decision-making.

Advanced dashboard systems integrate predictive analytics functions that allow investors to predict upcoming trends while actively managing potential problems like seasonal vacancies and expected maintenance costs. Dashboard tools that provide direct connections to external databases enable investors to automatically access real-time market data as well as tax records and demographic information, which helps in evaluating property values. Dashboard customizable alerts notify investors immediately when critical performance metrics surpass predefined limits, which helps them take timely action against potential risks. These advanced features make dashboard tools essential for dynamic investment management so stakeholders can confidently make informed decisions with better foresight.

Implementation Tip:

When setting up a dashboard or spreadsheet, label each metric clearly (e.g., "Rent Collected – June 202X"). This naming convention reduces confusion during reviews and aids any collaborators who need to interpret your data. Using standard "key fields" property name, address, monthly rent, and significant expenses facilitates portfolio growth because you can implement the same format for new investments.

Conducting Comparative Market Analysis (CMA):

Data collection becomes more manageable with proper tools, but market context interpretation remains an essential skill. By using Comparative Market Analysis (CMA), you can evaluate properties' current worth and future potential in their respective areas to craft improved pricing strategies and negotiation approaches. A Comparative Market Analysis (CMA) allows you to evaluate a property's worth and future potential in its area, which helps establish precise pricing methods and negotiation approaches.

• Finding Comparable Properties: The cornerstone of CMA is identifying "comps." Typically, these are properties that share various features such as location, square footage, property age, and properties sold or listed within the last few months. You can sense how your target property might fare on the market by assessing its listing prices or final sale amounts. Research through MLS and public record databases provides access to precise and updated comparative market data.

To broaden your Comparative Market Analysis, you must investigate extra property attributes that basic listings omit, including special amenities and neighborhood infrastructure improvements or local usage regulations. The analysis of changes in listing duration and price cuts helps reveal shifts in buyer behavior that indicate market trends toward cooling or heating. Combining detailed observations with traditional comps data enables investors to develop enhanced pricing approaches while evaluating offer competitiveness and gaining deeper insight into local real estate dynamics.

• Evaluating Market Trends: To validate your price range derived from comparable sales data, you must evaluate how supply and demand interact in the market. Analysts track indicators to determine market conditions, including the average listing duration of properties and neighborhood demographic transformations. Altos Research reports deliver advanced insights through detailed analysis of inventory levels, price fluctuations, and absorption rates.

Investors can improve their market analysis by tracking external elements, including local employment prospects and upcoming infrastructure developments, which have the potential to impact buyer preferences and price stability. Using broader economic and community developments in your analysis allows you to develop a more comprehensive understanding of future market directions. Utilizing Altos Research findings together with neighborhood growth trend observations helps investors refine their decisions about properties to invest in and react proactively to market changes.

Using Public Records: Publicly accessible data (e.g., prior sale prices, tax assessments) fills in important details missing from listings alone. Unusual price fluctuations or frequent sales within a brief timeframe suggest possible hidden problems with the property. Reviewing property tax records helps you understand continuing ownership expenses, which become crucial information when you intend to maintain the investment for an extended period.

Investors have the option to review permits and zoning documents alongside fundamental records to uncover any substantial changes to properties or existing code violations. Examining past renovations and expansions reveals insights into structural stability and can identify compliance problems. Additional analysis uncovers hidden risks beyond sales data and assists investors in making precise maintenance cost predictions for the future. Investors who combine building and zoning records with public data information develop a more comprehensive view of a property's lasting value and avoid future unexpected issues.

Imagine an investor, Carolina, who notices that a small apartment building in her target neighborhood has changed hands multiple times within just a few years. Concerned about why owners keep leaving the property, she consults municipal documents to find historical renovation details and records of pending city directives. Through this research, Carolina discovers that the property has been subject to costly repairs tied to outdated plumbing codes, which had not been fully resolved by previous owners. Armed with these findings, she can more accurately project ongoing repair costs, inform her lending partners about potential compliance expenses, and plan a realistic timeline for any necessary fixes ultimately making a more informed decision about whether to move forward with the acquisition.

Professional Appraisals: While a CMA is usually enough for initial evaluations, professional appraisals add credibility, especially if you seek financing. Appraisers use uniform criteria to assign a value to the property, helping confirm (or challenge) your CMA findings. Appraisals confirm proper pricing for lenders and partners to facilitate smoother negotiations in complex deals such as multi-unit buildings.

Take for instance, you want to buy a three-bedroom duplex located close to an area of fast commercial growth. Your CMA uncovers nearby properties of similar size that sold within the last six months, each commanding a roughly 10% higher price point than they did a year ago. Public records confirm consistent sale patterns, and market reports reveal a mild seller's market. These insights enable you to confidently approach the upper end of the offer range because ongoing neighborhood growth justifies a moderate premium.

Calculating ROI and Cap Rate:

CMA analysis establishes a property's price boundaries, but additional techniques remain necessary to calculate expected returns. Investors are able to evaluate performance with ROI and Cap Rate in order to make informed investment decisions.

ROI (Return on Investment):

The ROI determines the profit percentage your property makes in comparison to your initial investment sum.

Example: If you purchase a home for $200,000, put $20,000 into renovations, and sell it for $250,000, your total return is $30,000 ($250,000 minus $220,000). Dividing $30,000 by your initial $220,000 yields an ROI of roughly 13.6%. Investors often break down total return further, separating rental cash flow from appreciation to see which factor strongly drives profitability.

Cap Rate (Capitalization Rate):

Cap rate focuses on the relationship between net operating income (NOI) and the property's current value. A property's NOI covers all income (rent, parking fees, etc.) minus operating expenses (maintenance, taxes, insurance) but excludes debt service. The cap rate stands at 5% for a multi-unit property that produces an NOI of $15,000 and holds a valuation of $300,000. Cap rates provide a means for comparing properties or geographic areas, but higher rates can signal increased risk due to instability in their respective markets.

Trina evaluates a multi-unit property that presents an annual net operating income of $15,000 against an asking price of $300,000, which results in a 5% capitalization rate. Trina evaluates this property by comparing it to another building in an adjacent market, which advertises a marginally higher cap rate but suffers from greater tenant turnover rates and an irregular rent collection history. Trina needs to evaluate property stability and market conditions to determine if the consistent 5% cap rate of the first property outweighs the uncertain returns of the second property.

Best Practices:

*Ensure Data Accuracy: ROI and cap rate become distorted when inaccurate rent estimates combine with overlooked expenses, leading to faulty decision-making. Reducing calculation errors becomes possible when you verify your data sources, including lease terms, maintenance logs, and utility bills. Complete documentation of property expenses enables you to identify spending discrepancies across time frames, which increases the dependability of your financial forecasts.

*Review Often: Make sure to update these metrics on a regular basis whenever there are modifications to rent prices or when major repairs are completed or when local property values experience changes. By keeping ROI and cap rate calculations current with new data, you can identify market trends and prevent dependence on stale numbers. Periodic analysis of these metrics will cause you to reassess your property performance assumptions, which will help maintain alignment between your decisions and current market realities.

*Combine Metrics: ROI focuses on total gains, whereas the cap rate evaluates operational performance. Using both provides a more holistic view. Examining both figures together reveals essential information about sustained value growth and operational performance efficiency. When analyzing numerous properties concurrently, this dual evaluation approach allows investors to identify properties that deliver optimal stable income with maximum appreciation potential.

Investors enhance their analysis by applying stress-testing scenarios, such as unexpected rent declines or increased maintenance costs, to examine the sensitivity of each metric to sudden changes. These simulations, together with current market data, identify when an investment may become unprofitable or excessively risky to hold. Your investment strategy becomes more resilient when you anticipate various potential outcomes, which allows you to maintain both your short-term and long-term financial objectives.

Illustrative Scenario:

You purchase a small apartment complex for $500,000. After operating for a year, you realize $60,000 in annual rent minus $15,000 in expenses, resulting in $45,000 NOI. Thus, your cap rate is 9% ($45,000 / $500,000 × 100). If you financed a part of the property, you should also compute the ROI, factoring in the mortgage payments to see how well the leverage will amplify your returns.

Bringing It All Together:

Real estate's complexity demands systematic, tech-assisted approaches to property evaluation. We've demonstrated throughout this chapter that spreadsheet software, investment calculators, and mobile apps simplify the process of data gathering and calculations for everything from initial deal screening to determining your ROI. Comparative market analysis determines potential property value, while ROI and Cap Rate metrics demonstrate profitability. Implementing these tools and methods together allows you to convert a seemingly overwhelming market into an area of control through real data insights.

New investors typically struggle with connecting their current knowledge to essential concepts. Accessible spreadsheets, online calculators, and real estate applications help you approach deals confidently by leveling the playing field. Through continuous performance tracking provided by dashboards and advanced data-visualization tools, you can take action to prevent significant issues from developing. Together with the rigorous methodology of CMA and the clear insights provided by ROI/Cap Rate metrics, they form a powerful toolkit that protects your capital while aligning your investments toward long-term wealth creation.

These tools will develop over time to provide advanced analytics and predictive modeling capabilities. Keep your strategy flexible to adapt to technology and market dynamic changes. Your ability to adjust and refine your investment techniques keeps you prepared to succeed in real estate investment and enables you to guide your financial future using updated modern resources.

Ch. 7 - Understanding and Mitigating Risks

Effective real estate investors understand potential risks while learning how to manage them effectively. Real estate investment has the potential for substantial financial profit, yet it demands meticulous planning to overcome its fundamental challenges (Side Hustle Wealth Builders). The financial outcomes of property investors depend significantly on various risks encountered during the investment process, which encompasses market instability alongside tenant management challenges, legal limitations, and financial overextension. Real estate investors who want to expand their wealth and protect it need to understand how to identify and minimize potential risks. Investors build a strong and lasting portfolio when they identify vulnerabilities early and develop solutions before problems arise.

This chapter focuses on several strategies that help reduce the risks found in real estate businesses. This section teaches you how to spread investments over multiple property types and regions to prevent a single weak area from affecting your overall business plan. This section emphasizes the importance of performing complete due diligence on properties, which helps avoid expensive errors by demonstrating how inspections and research play a vital role. The discussion will include creating financial reserves to mitigate unexpected challenges while protecting continuous business activities and maintaining stability. The chapter demonstrates how expert assistance from real estate agents and attorneys to property managers enhances decision-making processes while minimizing errors. We examine insurance policies together with asset protection structures that protect investors from liabilities and various disruptions. A thorough understanding of these financial instruments will enable real estate investors to confidently handle investment complexities while at the same time being able to achieve enduring growth and success.

Identifying Common Real Estate Risks:

Real estate investment success depends on an investor's ability to identify and control the various risks that will be encountered in the market. Investors aiming for sustained success must identify typical real estate risks since the industry contains numerous uncertainties that affect both profitability and asset value. Investors need to keep up with macroeconomic trends since market downturns, together with rising interest rates and inflation levels, affect property values and rental demand. Investors face regulatory risks from zoning law changes, tax policy adjustments, and tenant protections, which make their investments more uncertain and demand continuous compliance to prevent legal issues. Financial and operational difficulties may arise from interpersonal risks that involve unreliable tenants, untrustworthy contractors, or problematic business partners. Risk management becomes effective when investors perform comprehensive due diligence while keeping financial reserves and spreading their investments across multiple areas. Investors who actively find properties and are able to manage the risks can build more substantial portfolios and move through real estate market complexities with increased assurance. Maintaining readiness for various economic, regulatory, and interpersonal challenges helps to avoid disruptions and support continuous growth.

Market Risk:

Market risk arises from shifts in property values and public demand driven by several economic changes. Events like the COVID-19 pandemic clearly illustrate how quickly conditions can deteriorate, sometimes forcing property owners to lower prices or endure extended vacancies (Clardie, 2024).

The COVID-19 pandemic underscored how swiftly external factors can disrupt real estate markets, propelling investors into a state of heightened market risk almost overnight. Early lockdowns and social distancing measures halted in-person showings and delayed sales, forcing many sellers to lower asking prices or leave properties vacant longer to attract hesitant buyers. Consumer habits shifted notably toward remote work, affecting property demand patterns, with suburban homes appreciating in value and urban condos seeing reduced demand. Construction expenses rose because supply chain disruptions and labor shortages complicated both project timelines and investor budgets. These swift interconnected changes showed how real estate markets are sensitive to worldwide events, which requires investors to keep track of broad economic patterns while ensuring their strategies remain adaptable. To mitigate market volatility, investors should distribute their property investments between residential and commercial types across various locations. Monitoring interest rates and employment statistics together with consumer confidence data helps investors make better choices about buying, selling, or holding properties.

Tenant Risk:

The challenges presented by tenants, including irregular rent payments and property damage, create a substantial risk (Azibo, 2024). Background checks, income verification, and rental history reviews enable property owners to identify unsuitable renters through a rigorous screening process (Managing Rental Properties). Transparent lease agreements outline payment schedules and maintenance responsibilities while establishing dispute resolution procedures. Open communication between parties helps build strong relationships, leading to extended tenancy periods and reducing turnover expenses and legal conflicts.

Irregular Rent Payments and Property Damage: Frequent late payments not only cause immediate cash flow problems but they also prevent property owners from fulfilling their mortgage commitments and developing future investment strategies. Property damage exceeds normal wear-

and-tear when lease violations occur, leading to unforeseen repair bills and lengthy insurance procedures.

Background Checks, Income Verification, and Rental History: Prospective tenant screening confirms income sources and credit standing while identifying patterns of past eviction and irresponsible behavior. Owners who evaluate these factors create more precise risk assessments which decrease disputes while enhancing tenant satisfaction over time.

Transparent Lease Agreements: Owners who establish clear guidelines for reporting and dealing with maintenance problems achieve faster responses to property damage. Clauses that outline rules for guests, pets, and property changes create accountability and establish clear expectations which helps to prevent legal misunderstandings.

Open Communication: Landlords maintain awareness of tenant issues through regular interactions that include periodic check-ins. The early identification of issues enables proactive responses, which build mutual respect between parties and establish a setting that prevents harmful practices.

Integrating digital communication tools like tenant portals and messaging platforms helps property owners simplify maintenance requests and inspection scheduling. Accessible communication tools help diminish conflict resolution stress while building transparent property management relationships and maintaining tenant involvement in property upkeep. The stable and well-maintained environment results in benefits for both tenants and owners by discouraging disputes between parties while promoting lease renewals and enabling more consistent cash flow.

Legal and Regulatory Risk:

Investment strategies can face sudden disruptions from local ordinances, zoning regulations, and rent control policies. New regulations that limit short-term rentals or enforce stricter building codes will directly influence investor returns.

New York City's initiative to limit short-term rentals that were operated through platforms like Airbnb and similar others caused significant repercussions for local property owners and investors who depended on substantial nightly rates for rapid profit generation. Under tight regulations, many owners suddenly found themselves unable to legally rent out entire apartments for less than 30 days without meeting stringent criteria such as the host being present or the property meeting specific building codes. Investors expecting quick profits found their rental income decreased, which forced them to switch to long-term leases with lower monthly payments. Properties transferred to new owners no longer generate the financial returns they used to produce. Regulatory changes introduced complexities through administrative compliance requirements and potential penalties for noncompliance while illustrating how quickly property profitability can be affected.

Real estate lawyers provide legal updates through regular meetings that support strategic business decisions. Real estate networks and local government hearings provide businesses with advance notice about policy changes, enabling them to make proactive adaptations.

Financial Risk:

Financial overextension of leverage is a common danger for investors, particularly for those who are relying heavily on leverage. Although borrowing can magnify gains, it likewise accentuates losses if income declines or unexpected repairs arise. Practical cash flow management factoring in taxes, insurance, maintenance, and potential vacancies helps avoid undue strain. Reserving funds for emergencies (like structural damage or a spike in vacancy rates) can keep an investment afloat during lean times. Using conservative estimates when determining revenue and expenses will help limit possible cash flow limitations.

The implementation of different proactive investment strategies enables investors to maintain stability across a number of fluctuating real estate markets. You can build a more substantial investment portfolio through diversification combined with detailed due diligence and contingency planning, which leads to both portfolio growth and resilience.

Investors can attain diversification through investment distribution across multiple asset classes as well as different locations and tenant profiles. Home rental properties tend to deliver steady income streams, but commercial or industrial real estate often produces more significant revenue through extended lease contracts. When you combine multiple property types into a portfolio across different regions, you protect against economic downturns in any specific market. This diversified investment strategy protects cash flow while at the same time reducing the impact of unexpected market declines.

Due Diligence:

The profitability of a property heavily depends on its history and current condition. The multifaceted field of investment real estate reveals that property profitability depends mainly on its past history alongside its present state. Property history includes multiple aspects such as previous ownership details, records of renovations, and prevailing market trends throughout those times. A well-kept property with a record of steady occupancy shows potential for stable income to investors, but properties that have experienced frequent vacancies or significant structural problems throughout their history present investment risks.

The combination of neighborhood background checks, structural inspections, and financial history reviews reveals hidden issues in existing rental properties. During an initial inspection, outdated electrical and plumbing systems might escape detection, yet they represent expensive risks for future property owners. The current state of a property holds equal importance in determining its profitability. Contemporary infrastructure combined with modern amenities in excellent condition makes properties appealing to potential tenants who are happy to pay premium rental rates. Properties that need major repairs and renovations can become financially burdensome due to increased expenses alongside potential income loss while renovations are completed. Local market conditions, including rental demand, economic factors, and neighborhood developments, must be evaluated by investors since they influence both the current property value and future appreciation potential.

By verifying local ordinances, you can avoid legal complications like rental duration limits or property use restrictions. Preemptive measures and transparent negotiations enable you to prevent unexpected discoveries. A thorough understanding of historical and current property conditions is essential for investors to make informed investment decisions. Investors must complete thorough due diligence when evaluating potential investments, including property inspections, market analysis, historical performance evaluations, to assess potential returns and risks. Maximizing returns through strategic decision-making requires investors to follow a holistic approach to achieve long-term investment goals.

Building Financial Buffers:

Adequate cash reserves provide essential protection to handle unexpected expenses. By saving rental income, you can manage property repairs and tenant vacancies without needing to obtain expensive loans. The financial buffer protects you from making impulsive property sales during unfavorable market conditions. When you proactively budget funds specifically for maintenance fees, insurance, and taxes, you achieve stable financial management, enabling you to concentrate on growth opportunities.

The proper cash reserve percentage is critical in real estate investments to ensure financial stability while managing risks. Property owners should keep cash reserves that cover 3 to 6 months of operating expenses. The necessary operating expenses consist of mortgage payments, property taxes and insurance costs, maintenance, fees, and any additional regular expenses.

Investors usually reserve between 10% and 20% of the property's value as their cash reserve fund. The recommended percentage for cash reserves fluctuates depending on property type, market conditions, and personal financial circumstances. Investors in rental properties benefit from larger cash reserves because they can handle unexpected repair costs or periods when the property remains vacant.

Potential investors should evaluate the unique risks in their local real estate market. During unstable market conditions, businesses must maintain more significant cash reserves to protect themselves from possible financial declines. The fundamental principle involves maintaining adequate liquidity for effective investment management and preparation for unexpected events.

Professional Assistance:

Utilizing professional expertise enhances your risk management processes. Real estate professionals deliver market intelligence and establish negotiation strategies while monitoring industry trends in conjunction with legal advisors who explain contractual details and compliance requirements. Meanwhile, hiring a property manager offloads operational tasks finding and screening tenants, handling routine maintenance, and ensuring compliance so you can direct attention toward broader strategic objectives. These specialists supply credible knowledge that reduces guesswork and streamlines decisions.

For example, James successfully grew a single-family rental portfolio in his hometown until his attempt to purchase a multi-family property in another state exposed him to the complexities of an unknown market. He enlisted a local real estate agent to reduce risks and make educated decisions because the agent provided essential market information that led him to a high-demand area. James sought legal counsel from a real estate attorney to structure his property deal under an LLC and maintain local law compliance, which protected him from liabilities.

James also employed the services of a property management company to address the difficulties of remote management, which included tenant screening and rent collection, as well as maintenance responsibilities. The property produced a consistent cash flow because James employed a professional team to manage it. James expanded his real estate portfolio with confidence through expert guidance, which showed that successful real estate management relies not on solitary efforts but on building a team that helps you make decisions and maintain growth.

Insurance and Asset Protection:

All diversified investments that have undergone thorough research still contain unavoidable risks. Real estate investors need insurance and asset protection as critical defenses against unforeseen events and liabilities that can threaten their sustained profitability. Comprehensive property insurance policies such as landlord insurance, hazard insurance, and umbrella liability coverage can protect against damages caused by natural disasters, tenant-related issues, or unforeseen structural failures. Investors can protect their personal assets from legal actions and financial claims by holding investments through limited liability companies (LLCs) or trusts, which serve as a barrier against lawsuits and creditors' demands. Beyond traditional insurance, investors should also consider title insurance to guard against ownership disputes and fraudulent claims and business interruption insurance to cover lost rental income in case of catastrophic property damage. A comprehensive asset protection strategy requires both appropriate insurance policies and effective legal and financial planning to protect investment properties against unforeseen issues. Insurance and asset protection strategies help shield you from unexpected events, financial liabilities, or legal entanglements that might threaten your properties.

Property and Liability Insurance:

Real estate investors require property insurance to protect themselves from financial ruin caused by unforeseen property damage. Property insurance deals with damages caused by fire, theft, vandalism, or other incidents, typically covering the building's structure and its contents (Reed, 2024). Certain risks like floods or earthquakes often need supplementary policies, especially if you invest in high-exposure areas. Liability insurance offers protection when individuals get injured on your property or when a tenant's belongings become damaged during your management. Most lenders require borrowers to maintain renters' insurance coverage to protect their interests against catastrophic events.

Beyond structural repairs and stolen property protection from fire and vandalism, these policies may offer loss of rental income coverage to landlords when damage prevents property occupancy for a time. This feature benefits investors relying on rental income to pay mortgage payments and operating costs. Investors must carefully review insurance policy specifications, such as coverage details and exclusions, along with claim procedures because the nature of insurance policies continues to change, and they need protection that matches their distinct needs.

Regions susceptible to natural disasters, such as hurricane-threatened coastal zones and earthquake-prone fault-line regions, require supplementary insurance coverage. Since standard policies do not cover these risks, investors can protect themselves from severe financial losses due to natural disasters by purchasing additional insurance for flood, earthquake, or windstorm events. Property owners rely on liability insurance for personal injury claims and legal defense costs to protect themselves from lawsuits about accidents, structural defects, and tenant disputes. Financing conditions from lenders require borrowers to hold insurance, which protects lender collateral from disasters and emphasizes the need for complete coverage within real estate investment approaches.

Establishing LLCs or Trusts:

Formal legal structures, such as Limited Liability Companies (LLCs) or trusts, can further insulate personal assets from claims against specific properties (Insuring Property Held by a Trust or LLC | MMA, 2015). Should legal disputes or lawsuits arise, these entities help compartmentalize liability, protecting your broader portfolio. The strategies present tax benefits along with better asset distribution to family members. Precise documentation maintenance combined with proper insurance policy ownership by the correct entity helps avoid coverage denials and potential problems.

The following situation demonstrates how legal entities play an essential role in real estate investing by preserving wealth and liability protection to maintain long-term financial security.

As an experienced real estate investor, Michael owned rental properties in various neighborhoods. He protected his personal assets from legal risks by forming separate LLCs for each property, which allowed liability to stay isolated. This organizational method demonstrated its worth when an incident occurred at one of his apartment complexes.

A tenant encountered serious injuries after slipping on an icy sidewalk outside the building one evening. In a personal injury lawsuit seeking substantial damages, the tenant claimed that inadequate maintenance led to dangerous conditions. The property's holding within its own LLC protected Michael's personal savings and other properties from liability since only the assets inside the specific LLC faced risk exposure.

The LLC's proper insurance coverage absorbed all legal fees and potential settlement costs, protecting the owner from personal financial liabilities. There was no risk to Michael's complete asset portfolio, including his home and additional rental holdings, because the property was registered under his LLC instead of his personal name. His strategic use of LLCs to manage his investments protected his main portfolio while ensuring compliance with insurance regulations and legal standards.

As property values change due to renovation projects, market appreciation, or expansions your original insurance may no longer be sufficient. Maintaining appropriate coverage during calamities requires routine assessments of policy limits and endorsements (Reed, 2024). Organizations must prioritize policy reviews during the acquisition of new properties or the upgrading of existing properties. Adjusting insurance policies to match your portfolio's present-day conditions strengthens your protection against expensive disruptions.

Final Thoughts:

Real estate investment can yield substantial returns but requires careful oversight of industry-specific risks (Fix and Flip Loans). This chapter identified critical vulnerabilities, including market fluctuations and tenant conflicts, as well as regulatory uncertainty and financial pressure, and demonstrated methods investors can use to manage these risks. A strong defensive strategy emerges from employing portfolio diversification tactics alongside thorough property inspections and maintaining healthy cash reserves while obtaining professional support. Investment protection against unforeseen risks comes from insurance and the strategic selection of legal structures.

Detailed strategies function as solutions to resolve potential issues and build the groundwork needed for future development. Your capacity to maintain stability improves while you discover opportunities through vigilant threat monitoring and adaptive responses to changes. Competitive real estate management demands ongoing knowledge of regulatory changes and market shifts alongside tenant needs because the sector faces constant transformation. Striking a balance between calculated risks and diligent safeguards enables you to pursue sustainable long-term property investment success.

Side Hustles That Lead to Financial Stability - Side Hustle Wealth Builders. https://sidehustlewealthbuilders.com/side-hustles-that-lead-to-financial-stability/

Managing Rental Properties: 28 Best Areas To Master - Blog. https://blog.rentzap.com/managing-rental-properties/

Fix and Flip Loans: Fast Funding to Help You Maximize Property Returns - Kinked Press. https://kinkedpress.com/fix-and-flip-loans-fast-funding-to-help-you-maximize-property-returns/

Ch. 8 - The Role of Mentorship and Networking

Success in the real estate industry depends substantially on your willingness to participate in various mentorship programs and establish networking connections. Investors who take the time to network with experienced professionals usually gain vital information pertinent to their own strategic growth. Mentorship paired with networking forms a dynamic framework where guidance meets opportunity to empower individuals with enhanced confidence when tackling real estate market challenges.

This chapter examines how to identify and connect with mentors who can make a remarkable difference in your professional development. The training will teach you how to pinpoint potential mentors in your field and engage them with authentic intent. Our exploration will focus on the detailed networking aspects to build and sustain productive relationships while presenting strategies that help establish long-term connections leading to new business opportunities. Real estate endeavors that join industry events with online platform usage create supportive knowledge communities, which result in financial freedom and portfolio growth.

Finding a Mentor in the Industry:

The base foundation for real estate investment success is established through mentorship for aspiring investors. Newcomers receive guidance from experienced mentors who show them how to sidestep common errors and find new possibilities. When mentorship offers clear directions, it boosts learning speed and enhances decision-making abilities.

Mentors extend their roles beyond giving advice by offering structured growth pathways that help mentees polish their investment skills and comprehend real estate transaction complexities. Aspiring investors who study market trends and industry changes under an experienced mentor acquire valuable insights that would require years of trial and error to develop independently. The real estate market remains dynamic because economic trends, policy changes, and financing options continue to evolve. Through mentorship, investors develop the necessary skills to react to market changes successfully, which helps them maintain their competitive edge in a constantly evolving industry.

Mentors connect their mentees with essential professional networks made up of lenders, contractors, and legal advisors, which helps speed up their investment progression. The relationships established through mentorship offer functional benefits while simultaneously emphasizing relationship-building as a key factor for real estate achievements. A mentor with extensive connections enables access to advanced opportunities beyond fundamental learning, including partnerships in profitable deals and entry into exclusive investment groups.

Moreover, mentorship fosters confidence in decision-making. Many new investors demonstrate hesitation because they worry about potential financial losses and have doubts about property valuations and market opportunities. Mentor guidance eliminates doubts by confirming investment decisions through practical experience and evidence-based evaluations. Mentees develop proactive behaviors and show readiness to take advantage of opportunities while their ability to evaluate risks and returns strengthens.

Investor foundation improves through mentorship but only works well when mentees actively engage while asking insightful questions and applying what they learn. A successful mentorship requires mutual commitment where the mentee shows dedication and acts on guidance, which allows both mentor and mentee to gain from shared knowledge and experience.

Identifying Potential Mentors:

Begin your professional path by studying accomplished industry leaders with careers that match your professional goals. Locate professionals who have succeeded and built expertise in specific areas you're interested in, such as residential rentals, commercial properties, or niche markets. Seasoned professionals from the real estate industry can be found at professional associations, along with real estate seminars and forums. Observing industry leaders in action will help you assess their tactics to see if they align with your professional goals.

Beyond attending industry events, leveraging digital resources can be an effective way to identify and connect with potential mentors. Social media platforms such as LinkedIn, industry blogs, and real estate investment forums provide valuable insights into an expert's experience, investment philosophy, and recent achievements. Engaging with their content whether by commenting on their posts, sharing relevant articles, or participating in discussions can help establish a professional rapport before making direct contact. Additionally, many successful investors and real estate professionals host webinars, podcasts, or online courses, offering an opportunity to learn from them while also positioning yourself as an engaged and interested mentee. By proactively seeking out thought leaders in your area of interest and consuming their educational material, you demonstrate initiative and make it easier to establish a mentor-mentee relationship.

Networking within your local market is another powerful strategy to identify mentors who can provide hands-on guidance. Joining local real estate investment groups, attending property tours, and volunteering for real estate-related community events can place you in proximity to experienced investors and professionals. Many seasoned mentors appreciate mentees who show commitment through active participation rather than simply seeking advice. Building an organic relationship based on mutual interests and value exchange creates a foundation for a long-term mentorship. Rather than focusing solely on what a mentor can provide, consider how you can contribute whether through market research, digital marketing skills, or assisting in operational tasks. This reciprocal approach increases the likelihood of forming a meaningful connection and solidifies your position as a dedicated learner in the real estate space.

Approaching a Mentor:

Your introductory message to a potential mentor should show them your appreciation for their expertise and describe how their mentorship will benefit your personal growth. Investigate their professional background to understand their career path, along with their significant accomplishments. Frame your introduction around targeted questions or challenges you face this demonstrates seriousness and respect for their time. Mentors must establish authentic communication and prioritize helping people who demonstrate genuine interest and a desire to learn.

Your mentorship goals should be set by understanding the support your mentor can offer through their personal limits and their expert knowledge. Mentors utilize different approaches; some mentors deliver broad strategic direction, while others specialize in transactional advice and market insights. Monitoring your progress and staying aligned with set goals will require both parties to establish and follow a monthly call schedule along with quarterly meetings. Also, it may be necessary to get into the habit of spontaneous messages when required.

Providing consistent progress updates shows your dedication to your mentor's recommendations and your gratitude for their support. Equally important is the reciprocating value where possible: Offer your expertise in digital marketing solutions together with market research insights and cutting-edge technology tools to enhance their operational performance. The mutual exchange between parties helps maintain relationship balance and delivers benefits to each participant.

After establishing a solid connection, your mentor may present you to key industry leaders, which expands your professional network. Introductions through mentorship networks at events or through recommendations frequently unlock partnership opportunities that would typically remain inaccessible. These opportunities demand careful follow-through since they reflect your demonstrated skills and your mentor's validation.

Building Productive Relationships:

Real estate professionals who create strong connections achieve a more significant market presence and more transaction possibilities. Networking will enable you to develop a communal atmosphere that allows members to work together, using shared knowledge to reach collective success.

Aspiring professionals should attend industry events such as large expos and local investor meetups to network with established peers and veteran experts. Physical interactions provide profound experiences that digital engagements typically miss, creating opportunities for more personal future business connections. Be willing to join panels and participate in breakout sessions while maintaining an open-minded attitude during business discussions. Authentic interaction with different perspectives generates innovative thoughts and builds reliable relationships.

Social media sites such as LinkedIn and Facebook, together with niche real estate forums, expand your professional network across various geographic areas (Search Engine Marketing Can Increase...). Exchange ideas by sharing market trend articles and providing meaningful comments on posts while joining niche investment groups such as multifamily and commercial real estate. When you engage with peers on a regular basis, it will help showcase your valuable contributions, which will lead them to approach you for collaborative opportunities.

Even brief encounters, such as a five-minute seminar conversation or an online interaction, can become the foundation for lasting connections. You demonstrate respect and sincere interest in ongoing communication by sending personalized messages soon after your initial interaction. Point out detailed elements from your dialogue to indicate that you were actively engaged during your conversation. Regular follow-ups maintain momentum, which allows casual acquaintances to evolve into strong industry allies.

When people observe transparent behavior and mutual support throughout their interactions, a sense of trust begins to form between them. To build trustworthiness, organizations must fulfill their promises and communicate information clearly. Show consistent respect when it comes to the personal boundaries of others at all times. Be able to build stronger team connections by assisting team members with their difficulties and remembering to celebrate their achievements as well. Building trust will allow your businesses to create and form partnerships that will lead to sustained success.

Embracing a Long-Term Perspective:

Networking extends beyond simply accumulating contacts. This networking approach works toward establishing reciprocal relationships that stand the test of time. Provide assistance to others without expecting direct reciprocation and support initiatives that benefit everyone involved.

Embracing a long-term perspective in networking means recognizing that meaningful relationships in the real estate industry are built on trust, consistency, and mutual value over time. Successful investors and professionals build their network relationships by delivering authentic support and market insights while sharing beneficial resources with others. Individuals who focus on relationship-building by mentoring newcomers and collaborating with industry peers establish more dependable professional networks than those who prioritize immediate deals. Sustained professional networking enhances one's reputation and credibility, along with generating goodwill, which can result in unforeseen opportunities and strategic alliances or access to insider knowledge that is not available through standard means.

Investors who prioritize collective network success and generous actions become trusted partners who are first considered for new deals and investment opportunities. Investors who demonstrate selflessness create lasting bonds that pay off when peers who benefit from their generosity return the favor during unexpected opportunities.

Engaging in optimal networking, combined with sustained momentum, requires real estate investors to create strategies aligned with their investment goals. You want a strategic plan designed to convert casual meetings into meaningful partnerships that will propel your investment activities forward.

Establish your goals before participating in both in-person networking events and online platforms. Do you need to find information about how to finance commercial real estate projects? Looking to partner on a development project? Through targeted networking activities, you can create effective connections with professionals who share your interests, as noted by Evans (2024).

Authentic networking thrives when conducted in an environment of mutual support. Be willing to offer assistance when needed and share data on emerging markets. Connecting one's peers with helpful resources or simply brainstorming solutions to a current challenge will help build your self-esteem among the group. When you position yourself as a resource rather than just a receiver, trust builds swiftly, and referrals or potential deals flow more naturally to you (Team, 2022).

Local clubs, forums, and broader professional organizations online and offline will anchor you in communities dedicated to real estate progress. Participate actively by making comments when in group discussions, be willing to volunteer for event committees, or even give short presentations on your areas of expertise. This consistent involvement will set you apart as someone invested in collective learning.

Virtual conferences and webinars bring together investors from various countries beyond traditional in-person meetups. Remote networking expands your range of potential partners or mentors, especially when local real estate opportunities are scarce. Social media platforms like LinkedIn allow users to track and gauge their achievements and gather endorsements, which helps build credibility within industry networks (Step-by-Step Guide to Finding Jobs...).

Keeping connections alive over time requires regular interaction through comments on progress updates and article recommendations that they find helpful. Simple yet considerate acts help to strengthen relationships while maintaining open communication channels for future work together.

Summary and Reflections

Networking and mentorship are crucial foundations for real estate success because they combine individual guidance with group community strength. Through effective mentorship, you quickly master industry complexities, preventing errors and enabling strategic advantage within market trends. Networking functions as an active framework that distributes knowledge and resources while delivering new opportunities directly to your path.

Investors who actively pursue and develop mentorship connections establish reliable guidance that enhances their expertise and improves their decision-making abilities. Regular and genuine offline and online peer interactions produce valuable connections that lead to innovative business opportunities and partnerships while offering profound industry knowledge. When you actively pursue mentorship and peer connections with defined goals and mutual support, you will improve your market image and connect with a network of compatible professionals. Combining individual mentoring with group participation drives real estate investors to achieve lasting successes and build a growing network of achievements.

Search Engine Marketing Can Increase Your Site
Traffic & Rankings.
https://www.neomartek.com/what-we-
do/digital-marketing/sem.html

Step-by-Step Guide to Finding Jobs with Visa
Sponsorship in the USA: Your Path to Employment
Opportunities. https://kotuvo.com/step-by-step-
guide-to-finding-jobs-with-visa-sponsorship-in-
the-usa/

Ch. 9 - Expanding into International Markets

Global market entry enables international real estate investors to find exciting business opportunities while achieving portfolio diversification benefits. Due to globalization in the world economy, investors show a growing interest in cross-border acquisitions, which offer better profit potential and the thrill of entering new markets. The entrance to international markets brings unique challenges, including dealing with various legal systems and cultural differences that require a strategic and knowledgeable approach.

This chapter bestows readers an analysis of essential elements required for successful international real estate investments, starting with a summary of current global property trends that support informed strategic choices. This section provides an examination of the evaluation and mitigation strategies necessary for managing overseas market risks with a particular focus on political stability and currency fluctuations. A detailed examination of legal structures and cultural elements shows how experienced investors build effective local networks that generate trust and improve transaction efficiency. The chapter combines practical examples with expert analysis to create the necessary confidence and skills for taking advantage of international real estate opportunities while addressing sector-specific challenges.

Understanding International Real Estate Trends:

Analyzing regional economic indicators forms the essential foundation for discovering and capitalizing on profitable international investment opportunities. When it comes to international investing, local property values can experience dramatic shifts due to geopolitical events and trade agreements alongside currency fluctuations (PwC, 2024). Investors who understand market dynamics track changes in interest rates, employment figures, and inflation rates to find stable growth indicators that point toward promising investment returns. The comprehensive analysis approach identifies markets that demonstrate increasing demand while also revealing those that are overextended or approaching a decline.

Technological advancements and infrastructural development alongside macroeconomic indicators fundamentally influence international real estate trends. When governments fund smart city developments alongside digital infrastructure and green energy initiatives, they establish new investment paths that provide substantial long-term value. Regions that adopt blockchain technology for property transactions benefit from heightened transparency and operational efficiency, which draws foreign investors looking for secure and efficient property acquisition methods. The growth of co-living spaces, together with remote work developments, has led to increased demand for flexible housing solutions as cities that support digital nomads and expatriates experience faster property value increases. Investors who grasp changing market forces can strategically position themselves in areas where technological advancement leads to long-term real estate growth.

Shifts in population demographics, together with migration flows, create significant impacts on real estate market demands worldwide. Nations with favorable work visa policies or expanding industries attract skilled professionals, which causes property markets to experience higher demand for both residential and commercial spaces. The aging demographics in specific areas generate heightened interest toward healthcare real estate and assisted living facilities which provides specialized investment opportunities. Market-savvy investors who track demographic shifts can find sectors that are under-supplied and ready to expand while crafting portfolios that meet enduring market needs instead of passing trends. Investors improve their decision-making abilities through the integration of economic data, technological advancements, and demographic analysis, which helps them reduce risks and boost their international real estate profits.

Urbanization and Emerging Hotspots:

Many cities around the globe have experienced growth due to accelerated urbanization, which has created increased demand for housing, office spaces, and infrastructure facilities (Straits Research, 2024). Major cities such as Lagos, Mumbai, and Beijing demonstrate the ability of population growth and infrastructure improvements to transform real estate markets and create high-potential investment opportunities quickly.

An experienced real estate investor, Anna dedicated her property investments to established markets within the United States. She developed an interest in the burgeoning real estate regions fueled by swift urban expansion after participating in an international real estate conference. Her research on global real estate patterns led her to recognize Lagos, Nigeria, as a high-growth market because of its expanding population base and rising middle class supported by key infrastructure projects. Lagos presented her with accessible property entry options that promised strong value growth compared to the fully occupied markets she knew.

Anna performed a detailed market analysis to validate her choice by reviewing government-backed infrastructure projects along with migration trends and commercial development strategies. The ongoing railway expansion and development of a tech hub indicated a growing need for residential and mixed-use properties. She invested in a mid-tier apartment complex close to an expanding business district to attract young professionals and expatriates who wanted contemporary homes. The rental market expanded quickly while property values rose substantially, achieving investment performance that surpassed her previous experiences in her local market.

Anna's investment strategy proved effective by targeting the movement patterns of urban development. Her decision to pursue emerging global hotspots instead of mature markets with slower growth enabled her to benefit from higher returns, increasing rental demand, and long-term economic expansion. Through her understanding of key urbanization trends and infrastructure growth, she achieved lasting success in rapidly expanding real estate markets. By understanding these megatrends, investors can identify fast-developing regions that offer better opportunities than fully developed areas that grow at a slower rate.

Comparative Analysis and Technological Tools:

Being able to do a comparative market analysis remains vital for finding top international real estate sites. Regional comparisons of critical metrics, including rental yields, vacancy rates, and demographic patterns, help investors make better strategic decisions while avoiding saturated markets. Technology has also reshaped this process: Through data analytics, investors achieve enhanced forecasting accuracy and speed, while virtual reality (VR) creates opportunities for remote property viewing. New technology solutions eliminate logistical constraints, which enables investors to evaluate remote properties easily using fewer resources while gaining more confidence.

Real estate market analysis reached new levels of sophistication through AI's ability to analyze large data sets instantly which provides investors with precise tools to detect market trends and forecast property value changes. Predictive models for strategic investment decisions emerge from machine learning algorithms that analyze historical pricing patterns alongside local economic indicators and consumer behaviors. Blockchain technology increases transaction security through its decentralized system, which creates tamper-resistant property records that prevent fraud in international real estate transactions. These technological advancements provide enhanced transparency and simplify due diligence procedures, which helps investors move through international markets with improved confidence and operational efficiency.

Smart contracts combined with cloud-based property management systems have made cross-border real estate transactions easier by reducing intermediary involvement and transaction costs. Investors can instantly review property performance metrics along with lease agreements and market updates from digital platforms, which supports improved decision-making regardless of their location. The integration of Internet of Things (IOT) devices in property management systems boosts operational efficiency through features that allow remote building system surveillance and predictive maintenance planning while optimizing energy usage. Investors who make use of digital tools for real estate markets secure a competitive advantage through operational efficiencies and enhanced asset management, which leads to better returns on their global property investments.

Assessing Risks in Global Markets:

Property value fluctuations amid political turmoil or sudden policy shifts will often force investors to conduct comprehensive reviews of the government's historical performance and financial health. The dangers of inflation and recession demonstrate economic instability that leads to similar problems.

Global market risk levels depend on factors such as government stability, investment regulations for foreign entities, and variations in currency values. Foreign investors face strict property ownership rules in some countries that mandate special permits and local partnerships or require residency status for real estate purchases. Investors face legal uncertainty when sudden changes occur in foreign investment regulations due to leadership transitions or shifts in economic priorities. Fluctuations in local currency values cause real estate returns to vary because international buyers face either reduced gains or increased costs due to currency exchange volatility. To secure financial stability, investors must protect their portfolios from currency risks through the use of multi-currency accounts and forward contracts, as well as investing in dollar-pegged economies.

A comprehensive assessment of long-term investment risks requires knowledge of demographic patterns and infrastructure stability. Population growth and employment rates, together with migration patterns, determine the demand levels for housing and commercial real estate in international markets. Regions experiencing aging populations or declining birth rates see housing market reductions that persist over time, whereas fast-growing middle-class populations with workforce expansion create sustainable investment opportunities. The strength of markets in maintaining economic growth during external disruptions depends on the quality of infrastructure investments, including transportation networks, technology hubs, and energy systems. Investors who evaluate socioeconomic and infrastructural indicators can protect their assets from risks and invest in regions that demonstrate strong growth potential over the long term. A comprehensive analysis of political systems and macroeconomic indicators reveals how well a region can withstand market disruptions, especially for investments that span multiple years.

Market Volatility and Diversification:

Real estate markets inherently fluctuate in cycles, and international forays add another layer of complexity (elliott.troop@ipglobal-ltd.com, 2024). By spreading investments across multiple countries or property types, investors dilute the impact of a local downturn in any single area. Historical data on boom-bust patterns can guide timing decisions, indicating whether short-term speculation or longer-term strategies are more viable in a given region.

Investors who distribute their assets across different geographical markets reduce their exposure to localized economic declines while seizing opportunities from diverse economic cycles. One nation might undergo a real estate boom because of economic growth or infrastructure improvements, while another nation encounters a reduction in real estate activity due to regulatory changes or currency devaluation. Investors who distribute their assets among markets with distinct growth patterns achieve a portfolio that remains steady despite economic fluctuations. Investing across multiple property types, including residential, commercial, industrial, and mixed-use real estate, helps protect investors from failures in any one market segment. Tourism-dependent short-term rental properties often face challenges during global travel disruptions but logistics and warehousing properties experience growth because of rising e-commerce demand.

Investors who incorporate real estate investment trusts (REITs) along with alternative asset types into their portfolios benefit from international market access because these investments require less capital and provide better liquidity options. Publicly traded REITs enable investors to spread their risk across numerous properties in global locations without requiring them to own those properties directly. Private equity real estate funds combined with real estate crowdfunding platforms enable investors to gain access to booming markets while avoiding the necessity of direct property management. Investors achieve better returns and maintain market response flexibility through the integration of conventional real estate investments with new financial tools. Through thorough research and data-driven decision-making, financial institutions maintain long-term stability and profitability for international real estate portfolios that remain stable through economic changes.

Currency Risk and Exchange Strategies:

Investors may notice substantial impacts on their returns from exchange rate fluctuations during profit repatriation (Read 2024). Foreign investors can benefit from an appreciating local currency, which increases their gains, but if the currency devalues, their profits will decrease. Investors can protect their finances from market volatility by leveraging currency hedging tools like forwards, futures, and options. The protection of portfolio performance depends on understanding currency trends combined with transactions in stable currencies whenever practicable.

When foreign currency rises against your home currency, you may achieve conversion gains beyond original estimates, which leads to significant portfolio return enhancement. When a local currency loses value, it reduces profit margins, which leads to diminished gains once funds are transferred back to the home country. Investors use currency hedging instruments like forwards, futures, or options to fix or offset exchange rate changes throughout a set time frame to protect against these risks. The practical application requires analysis of future cash flows and market trends to establish proper hedge levels and timings, which specialized foreign exchange advisors and financial institutions can refine.

Portfolio performance receives additional stability from the consistent monitoring of international currency markets along with transactions in stable currencies such as the euro and U.S. dollar. Systematic risk monitoring alongside precise instrument selection and strategic investment timing enables investors to diminish currency fluctuations' impact on international returns.

Legal and Regulatory Complexities:

Unlike local investing, foreign ownership requirements and tax regulations can demonstrate substantial differences when combined with compliance regulations and laws. Some nations impose restrictions that determine which property types foreign nationals can purchase and the extent of ownership rights available to them. International real estate investment faces a range of legal and regulatory challenges that extend past ownership limitations and tax requirements, including currency regulations and profit repatriation, as well as variable government policies, which may affect long-term investment stability.

Some nations implement capital controls to limit financial transfers and require foreign investors to establish local partnerships or meet residency requirements to purchase property. Investors from foreign nations need to understand that zoning laws and building regulations differ significantly from their own countries' standards and, combined with environmental regulations, can lead to costly legal disputes or project slowdowns when not adequately examined.

Because of these complexities, experts such as local legal counsel, tax professionals, and regulatory advisors become necessary partners to maintain compliance and avoid unexpected problems. Investors who understand global real estate laws protect their assets while positioning themselves to achieve smoother transactions and long-term success. Local legal experts working with strong due diligence processes offer compliance certainty and protection from regulatory errors. Completing this step protects stakeholders from hidden clauses and unfamiliar administrative processes that could jeopardize whole deals.

David, who invests in real estate from America, recognized a chance to grow his holdings when he acquired a beachfront property in Bali, Indonesia. The location of the property in a tourist-rich area made it seem like a beneficial short-term rental investment because more international visitors were looking for places to stay in private residences. David made the purchase decision because he trusted his research and anticipated substantial returns while believing the process would mirror his past U.S. real estate transactions.

David faced unexpected legal difficulties immediately after completing his property deal. Indonesian law forbids foreign individuals from holding freehold property titles but permits them to obtain properties through leasehold contracts that adhere to strict terms. The nation's property laws mandate that foreign investors create a local business entity or choose nominee ownership, requiring detailed legal structuring to secure long-term property rights. During his attempt to move rental income to his U.S. bank account, he encountered unforeseen capital restrictions that limited profit repatriation to a specific amount, resulting in extra taxes and processing delays.

After David recognized his error, he consulted both a property attorney and a tax specialist, who assisted him in restructuring his financial strategy. Legal advisors instructed him to establish a foreign-owned company registered as PT PMA to legally own the property and manage short-term rentals according to Indonesian laws. The additional paperwork and compliance measures proved necessary to protect his investment over time and facilitate legal earnings repatriation.

PT PMA represents (Perseroan Terbatas Penanaman Modal Asing), meaning Foreign Investment Limited Liability Company in Indonesia. A PT PMA represents a legal structure that permits foreign investors to establish and manage companies in Indonesia, including real estate operations, when specific criteria are satisfied. Through PT PMA establishment, foreign investors gain access to leasehold property acquisition, rental business management, and profit repatriation within Indonesian investment law frameworks.

Through his experience, David demonstrated how essential legal due diligence is when investing internationally in real estate because handling ownership laws and compliance requires professional expertise.

Navigating Legal and Cultural Challenges:

Distinct legal regulations govern land transactions and buildings, as well as environmental standards in every nation. Some regions require non-resident owners to obtain special permits while imposing strict rules for short-term rental operations. Knowledge of these regulations helps prevent legal conflicts and ensures contracts remain legally enforceable. Property ownership rights are divided into three main categories: freehold ownership, leasehold arrangements, and collective ownership models. Investors who comprehend different types of property ownership are able to protect their ability to develop and sell properties.

Each country maintains unique legal frameworks that dictate land transactions, building permit requirements, and environmental standards. Certain areas mandate that non-resident property owners secure special permits and establish stringent operating guidelines for short-term rentals. Being informed about regulations helps avoid legal disputes and maintains the enforceability of contracts. The three primary categories of property ownership rights consist of freehold ownership, leasehold arrangements, and collective ownership models. Understanding various property ownership structures enables investors to maintain their rights to develop and sell real estate.

Freehold Ownership:

The absolute and unlimited authority provided by freehold ownership makes it the safest and most wanted form of property ownership. The freehold ownership arrangement ensures that property owners keep both the land and any buildings on it indefinitely while operating under only standard zoning and regulatory laws. Long-term investors find freehold properties appealing because they permit unrestricted development opportunities and allow wealth-building through property appreciation while enabling ownership transfer without government restrictions. Some nations place limitations on foreign investors acquiring freehold property, which necessitates local residency status or business alliances with domestic firms for complete ownership rights. Investors must consider inheritance laws and property taxes because some areas apply significant taxation on foreign-owned freehold properties, which can affect long-term returns.

Leasehold Arrangements:

Under leasehold property ownership, an individual or entity obtains the right to use land or buildings according to a fixed time limit, which generally varies between 30 to 99 years based on an arrangement with the freehold owner who maintains overarching control of the property. High-demand urban centers frequently make use of leasehold arrangements that enable large landowners like governments or institutions to lease out property development and operational rights to private investors through fixed-term leases. Leasehold ownership grants access to prime real estate at reduced initial costs compared to freehold purchases. Still, it includes risks related to lease expiration dates and the terms of renegotiations, along with increasing ground rent fees. A property's market value tends to decrease when the lease period nears its end, which restricts resale opportunities unless a lease extension occurs. To protect long-term financial plans, investors must thoroughly evaluate renewal clauses and exit strategies to avoid unexpected interruptions.

Collective Ownership Models

Collective ownership means multiple people or organizations jointly holding property through a common management system, frequently appearing in cooperative housing and other real estate investment collectives. This model requires owners to share responsibility for maintaining common areas and making decisions together while rules are established by homeowners' associations or through co-op boards and investment syndicates. Through collective ownership, investors can pool resources for high-value properties while mitigating risks but must strictly follow community agreements and regulatory requirements. Investors must understand bylaws and voting rights and anticipate restrictions regarding renovations, rental operations, and resale conditions. Conflicts between co-owners or governing entities can generate legal battles or economic challenges, which makes conducting thorough due diligence essential before joining a collective ownership system.

Investors who comprehend these three primary property ownership structures can make strategic choices about markets and legal frameworks that match their investment objectives to achieve continuous stability and profitability while maintaining compliance across various global real estate markets.

Cultural Awareness and Negotiation:

The distinct negotiation methods, styles, communication choices, and local business mannerisms are heavily influenced by cultural norms. Strategies deemed routine in one context may be viewed as aggressive or disrespectful in another. Investors who invest in learning local customs and approaching deals with sensitivity often see smoother transactions and stronger partnerships.

Imagine an American real estate investor, Alex, traveling to Tokyo to negotiate a large commercial property deal with a Japanese developer. Coming from a background where deals are often conducted swiftly and directly, Alex prepares to use a straightforward, somewhat assertive approach to close the agreement quickly.

Upon arrival, however, Alex notices the developer's team is focused on building a relationship before discussing specifics. They begin the meeting by formally exchanging business cards, bowing instead of shaking hands, and taking time to inquire about Alex's journey and background. When Alex attempts to speed through the initial discussions asking bluntly about price and contract terms he senses an undercurrent of discomfort on the developer's side.

Rather than confronting him directly, the Japanese team responds by carefully avoiding overt disagreement. They continuously circle back to broader corporate goals and politely request more time to deliberate. Their primary focus remains on reaching an agreement and protecting reputations because any hint of discord or rapid decision-making threatens their collaboration. Understanding the importance of cultural dynamics, Alex adapts his strategy by demonstrating patience while asking about long-term goals and participating in social interactions that validate the group's set hierarchy.

The trust between Alex and the developer's team builds steadily through his culturally sensitive approach. The project's results, which align with Alex's goals, emerge after a more extended period than he first expected from the developer's team.

Alex secures a successful negotiation result and builds a long-term business relationship with the developer through adherence to Japanese cultural norms for harmonious communication and indirect negotiation methods, demonstrating cultural standards' importance in shaping negotiation tactics. Successful international partnerships depend on understanding cultural nuances like proper greeting formality and negotiation pacing to build essential trust.

Engaging Local Experts:

Property-related support is provided by real estate professionals alongside legal experts and consultants. Real estate experts assist clients with property valuations and growth opportunity identification while making sure all legal documentation requirements are fulfilled.

Let us take a look at this example: James, an established real estate investor from the U.S., intended to expand his property holdings by purchasing a beachfront rental property situated in Thailand. While exploring investment options, he recognized a luxury villa priced competitively as a perfect opportunity because the area had an expanding tourism sector, which interested him. James was prepared to complete his transaction because he relied on his research analysis.

Before completing the purchase agreement, James chose to speak with a real estate attorney who specialized in foreign investment transactions. The attorney identified multiple overlooked legal issues as soon as he reviewed James's plans. James could not legally take ownership of the land as Thai law prevents non-citizens from directly purchasing property. The attorney detailed alternative investment options, which included creating a Thai Limited Company and negotiating a long-term lease with the property owner. The attorney found out about secret zoning restrictions, which would have stopped James from using the villa as a short-term rental as intended for his investment.

With the help of his local attorney's expertise, James managed to sidestep an expensive error while developing a legal investment approach that let him earn money while following Thai regulations. A local professional with deep legal knowledge proves essential to overcoming legal challenges and regulatory obstacles for successful international real estate deals.

Professionals deliver assistance with regulations and act as cultural intermediaries who bridge language and etiquette gaps. Working with experts allows faster deal closure and reveals critical local contacts, including developers and tenants needed to maximize financial returns. Utilizing local expertise enables investors to prevent costly errors and accelerate market entry.

International Agreements and Bilateral Treaties:

Grasping bilateral and multilateral treaties can lead to more efficient international real estate deals because it minimizes legal issues and financial risks. For example, many countries have established double taxation treaties to ensure investors are not taxed twice (once in the source country and again in their home country) on the same income. Successful exploitation of these agreements requires comprehensive knowledge of all involved parties' tax regulations and an understanding of how deductions and credits combined with tax rate differences impact the ultimate profit from property investments.

International arbitration clauses that refer to global legal standards, including the UN Convention on Contracts for the International Sale of Goods (CISG), present a neutral dispute resolution framework to avoid lengthy legal battles in unfamiliar jurisdictions. Incorporating these provisions at the beginning of contracts will establish a straightforward process to resolve potential conflicts that will benefit both parties. Using this method will lead to better negotiation outcomes and decrease legal expenses and time spent resolving disputes in court if issues emerge.

Furthermore, investors who proactively incorporate treaty provisions into their investment structures for instance, through carefully chosen holding companies domiciled in treaty-friendly jurisdictions can experience fewer regulatory hurdles when transferring or repatriating funds. This structure provides protection against unexpected political or economic changes through international agreements that control property rights and capital movement. Real estate investors who methodically evaluate treaties and embed them into contractual agreements along with corporate structural adjustments achieve efficient border-spanning operations with uniform outcomes. Including these agreements in investment frameworks helps reduce operational conflicts and generate consistent results.

Concluding Thoughts:

International real estate investment provides numerous opportunities for growth in both emerging markets and established cities, as well as enhances portfolio diversity with better return prospects. The benefits of international real estate investment come with increased responsibilities because investors need to navigate through complex legal systems while understanding diverse cultural and financial environments. To maintain profitability in global real estate investment, thorough market analysis alongside political and economic diligence and careful currency fluctuation monitoring are essential.

Building genuine local relationships and demonstrating cultural understanding during cross-border negotiations are essential elements alongside other transaction aspects. Real estate investors who combine analytical rigor with open-minded adaptability will unlock extensive opportunities in international markets. Investors who combine VR and data analytics with local knowledge develop risk management skills and achieve global real estate strategy benefits through comprehensive analysis.

Global investment has become more straightforward due to technological progress and financial modeling but relies on strategic execution and direct involvement with local markets for sustained success. Investors need to cultivate a flexible approach to successfully maneuver through the distinct economic policy changes and real estate cycles and regulations that exist in foreign markets compared to their home markets. Direct connections with property managers and local developers, along with market analysts, provide investors with direct information about market developments and new investment possibilities. Investors can enter high-growth markets with reduced direct exposure by utilizing international financial structures such as Real Estate Investment Trusts (REITs) and joint ventures, which act as alternative entry points.

Thriving in international real estate requires investors to maintain a balance between risk management and opportunity identification. High-performing investors perform thorough due diligence and invest in various regions to protect themselves from market fluctuations after doing basic market research. Real estate investors who persistently enhance their strategies while merging conventional investment practices with current technological methods build enduring wealth throughout global markets. Real estate investors who actively adjust to regulatory changes and technological innovations while responding to evolving consumer demands will secure long-term growth opportunities in the worldwide market.

Ch. 10 - Harnessing Technology in Real Estate Investing

Advancements in technology have revolutionized real estate investing by improving transaction efficiency and property management capabilities to enable data-driven decision-making. Real estate professionals optimize investment strategies and customer experiences by using innovative solutions that range from predictive analytics to artificial intelligence and innovative property management tools.

Investors must stay ahead of technological advancements as the industry continues to embrace and maintain competitiveness. This chapter examines how real estate investing is being transformed through technological innovations such as property management software advancements and big data for decision-making alongside artificial intelligence growth and virtual reality property marketing applications. With technological advancements, investors must stay ahead of the curve to remain competitive. This chapter investigates how technology transforms real estate investing through property management software improvements and significant data decision-making impacts while investigating AI's rising influence and virtual reality's application in property marketing. Additionally, we will examine cybersecurity risks, best practices for tech implementation, and strategies for future-proofing real estate businesses in an increasingly digital landscape.

Technological Tools for Property Management:

Modern property management technology enables landlords, real estate professionals, and investors to optimize their operations while improving tenant satisfaction. The latest technology for property management allows landlords and real estate professionals to streamline operations and enhance tenant satisfaction simultaneously. The real estate sector has embraced digital transformation to use technology-based solutions to reduce operational costs and improve tenant engagement while optimizing workflows (Document Management System for Real Estate). Property managers and investors can supervise their portfolios efficiently by automating rental payments and adopting predictive maintenance tools to lower administrative burdens.

Innovative property management platforms support operational efficiency while offering features like tenant communication portals alongside automated lease renewals and AI-driven vacancy monitoring. These tools improve tenant experiences through immediate maintenance response times and digital documentation while offering self-service options. Real-time insights from data analytics embedded in these platforms provide detailed information on rental trends, occupancy rates, and cash flow performance, which helps investors make informed decisions while reducing guesswork.

The real estate sector's adoption of digital transformation has made technology-based solutions indispensable for workflow optimization and operational cost reduction while boosting tenant relationships. By automating rental payments and leveraging predictive maintenance tools, property managers and investors can effectively oversee their portfolios while reducing administrative burdens.

Automation of Rental Payments and Lease Management:

Automated rental payment systems represent a significant advancement in property management because they ensure that landlords receive payments on time.

The system enables tenants to complete their rent payments through an uncomplicated process. Tenants can complete their rent payments through online payment portals or mobile applications using credit cards, bank transfers, or digital wallets. The automation of late payment reminders through these platforms minimizes payment delays and enhances cash flow reliability for property owners.

Through the digital transformation of lease documents and automated alerts for rent escalation and lease renewals, these systems increase operational efficiency. These tools enable landlords to receive prompt lease renewal and contract expiration notifications, which assist them in strategically managing vacancies to sustain high occupancy levels. AI-powered lease tracking systems utilize historical rental data to develop pricing strategies that match current market conditions.

Predictive Maintenance and Smart Property Monitoring:

Predictive maintenance technology is transforming how property managers handle repairs and upkeep. By integrating Internet of Things (IoT) sensors and AI-driven analytics, property management platforms can detect potential maintenance issues such as HVAC system inefficiencies, plumbing leaks, or structural wear before they escalate into costly repairs. Building sensor data is collected continuously by these systems, which notify property managers about performance abnormalities while facilitating early maintenance planning.

Smart thermostats analyze energy usage to adjust temperature systems according to user presence and decrease both utility expenses and tenant discomfort. Water leak detection sensors enable the early identification of pipe leaks, which prevents significant damage and expensive repair work. Data-driven maintenance practices extend critical building systems' operational life while improving tenant satisfaction by resolving maintenance issues before they lead to disruptions.

Integration with Smart Building Technologies:

Today's property management systems connect with smart building technologies to provide landlords and investors with a unified platform for monitoring energy usage alongside security access controls and environmental conditions. The use of smart locks enables landlords to manage access privileges for maintenance personnel or tenants from a distance without needing to exchange physical keys. Through mobile apps, users gain the ability to track security cameras and operate access systems in real time, which enhances building safety.

The use of the Internet of Things (IoT) technology in property management has transformed asset monitoring and maintenance for landlords. Connected devices and smart sensors provide real-time monitoring of utility consumption and system operations, which help identify potential problems like water leaks and HVAC failures before they turn into expensive repairs. The new technological improvements lead to decreased operational costs while simultaneously enhancing energy efficiency and the sustainability of properties that appeal to environmentally aware tenants. Real estate investors and property managers can achieve long-term portfolio growth alongside enhanced tenant retention and increased profitability through the adoption of advanced technologies in competitive markets.

Automated climate control systems adapt room temperatures depending on occupancy, which delivers energy savings and lowers operational costs. When property management platforms integrate these technologies, they establish a comprehensive system that streamlines building management while providing tenants with a technologically advanced living experience.

Enhanced Tenant Communication and Service Requests:

The tenant experience directly influences property retention rates, while technological advancements transform landlord-tenant communication methods. AI-powered chatbots on property management platforms deliver immediate answers to tenant queries about lease terms, maintenance requests, and property policies. The round-the-clock virtual assistants both engage tenants more effectively and lessen property managers' workloads by managing common inquiries.

Mobile apps designed for tenants allow people to submit service requests quickly while enabling them to monitor repair progress in real time and provide feedback about the work completed. The streamlined process produces better tenant satisfaction while improving operational transparency through centralized documentation of all communications.

Scalability for Portfolio Growth:

When expanding portfolios without essential technology support, real estate investors face overwhelming property management challenges. Through a single dashboard, scalable property management solutions enable landlords to track multiple assets by combining financial reports with maintenance schedules and tenant records. The systems integrate with cloud storage, which makes documents and transaction records available from anywhere. Utilizing cloud storage systems for documents and transaction records enables investors to access their information from any location, which allows them to manage properties remotely while maintaining operational efficiency. Centralized operations enable these platforms to minimize duplicate tasks and tracking mistakes while improving daily property supervision, facilitating investment expansion with minimal administrative work.

Institutional investors and large-scale property managers use AI-driven analytics to monitor portfolio performance, market trends, and rental demand fluctuations to assess profitability and operational inefficiencies. Investors use predictive insights tools to estimate cash flow patterns and recognize underperforming assets while basing their property acquisition and divestment decisions on data analysis. The automated tenant management system that features AI leasing assistants and virtual property tours improves occupancy rates and expedites both tenant onboarding and lease renewals. Modern property management technology is essential for investors because it delivers automated administrative functions, financial tracking, and investment metric analysis to enhance profitability, reduce risk exposure, and maintain portfolio expansion over time in competitive markets. The scalability of modern property management technology becomes essential for investors who wish to improve their returns and reduce administrative burdens.

To sum it up, contemporary property management technology has transformed the way landlords and real estate professionals operate and maintain properties while benefiting investors. The combination of automated payment systems and predictive maintenance with smart building integrations and AI-driven tenant engagement leads to improved efficiency and reduced costs while simultaneously enhancing tenant experiences. Real estate professionals must utilize digital tools to maintain their competitive edge as technological advancement progresses in the market.

Integration with Accounting and CRM Systems:

Modern property management software extends beyond rent collection and maintenance tracking by enabling smooth integration with accounting systems, such as QuickBooks, alongside customer relationship management platforms. Investors benefit from this integration by automating financial reporting processes while simultaneously tracking expenses in real time and enhancing communication with tenants and property managers. Unified dashboards break down information barriers so that leasing, maintenance, and financial oversight teams within property management can access consistent and current data.

Cybersecurity and Data Privacy Considerations:

The increasing storage of sensitive data by property management systems has made cybersecurity an essential priority. Modern property management systems require crucial security measures, including encryption and multi-factor authentication, along with following data protection laws like GDPR and CCPA. To protect against data breaches, investors and landlords should put tenant payment information, lease contracts, and financial documents at the top of their security priorities. By utilizing cloud storage together with secure backup systems, organizations can safeguard essential documents from cyberattacks and unexpected data loss.

Proactive cybersecurity strategies serve as essential tools to stop unauthorized access and system vulnerabilities beyond encryption and multi-factor authentication methods. Organizations detect digital infrastructure vulnerabilities through consistent security audits and penetration testing, which keeps security procedures current. Educational programs for employees and tenants about phishing attacks, secure password management, and document handling help minimize human error that causes data breaches. Property managers can protect sensitive tenant and financial information by setting up role-based access controls to grant data access strictly to authorized staff members.

AI-based threat detection systems have become essential for property management security because cyber threats continue to develop. Real-time network monitoring systems detect suspicious activity and block breaches from expanding into full-blown incidents. Blockchain technology serves as an emerging solution in real estate to secure transactions and payment records through tamper-proof ledgers that maintain data integrity. Advanced cybersecurity measures help landlords and investors protect tenant data while maintaining regulatory compliance and building trust with renters and stakeholders to achieve operational stability in the digital real estate market.

Big Data and Predictive Analytics in Real Estate Investing:

Real estate investment strategies have evolved due to large-scale data analysis capabilities, which allow investors to transition from intuition-based decisions to accurate data-driven methodologies. Big data offers exceptional market analysis capabilities by tapping into the extensive datasets composed of both structured and unstructured information, such as property valuations, rental patterns, and demographic changes alongside economic signals. Investors who use the insights provided by big data to guide their decisions can pinpoint new opportunities while minimizing risks and enhancing asset performance accuracy.

Predictive analytics extends beyond market identification to provide real-time risk evaluations, which assist investors in forecasting changes in property demand alongside interest rates and rental pricing trends. Investors utilize machine learning models to identify small market changes, enabling them to accurately time their property purchases and sales and rental adjustments. The analytic tools evaluate various elements, including crime statistics, infrastructure improvements, and population movements, to deliver a detailed view of investment possibilities over the long term. Predictive modeling enables real estate professionals to strategically manage their pricing approaches, tenant acquisition plans, and property improvements instead of relying on reactive decision-making.

Big data strengthens portfolio diversification by enabling investors to assess numerous markets simultaneously while discovering connections among different asset classifications. Investors can create a well-balanced portfolio by analyzing historical transaction data in conjunction with current economic indicators, which helps them allocate investments between rapidly growing sectors and dependable cash-generating assets. Automated valuation models (AVMs) utilize big data to deliver immediate and precise property appraisals, diminishing the need for conventional valuation practices. The synergy between big data and predictive analytics gives investors the tools to optimize their long-term plans and boost asset performance while holding their place at the forefront of an ever-changing real estate market.

Real-Time Market Analysis for Smarter Investment Decisions:

Investors who utilize big data obtain real-time market insights, which enable them to respond quickly to economic changes, demand shifts, and neighborhood development patterns. Conventional market research methods depended on past sales figures that frequently became obsolete, resulting in lost opportunities and incorrect risk assessments. In contrast, modern AI-driven analytics track live property listings, rental vacancies, mortgage rates, and local economic conditions, giving investors an up-to-date snapshot of a market's performance.

For example, if an area sees a sudden surge in job growth and population influx, big data analytics can flag the location as a potential hotspot for residential investment. Investors should respond to signs of rising foreclosure rates or declining consumer spending by taking preventive actions to avoid risky markets and modifying pricing strategies.

Risk Reduction Through Data-Driven Forecasting:

Big data is most valuable in real estate investment because it helps discover patterns indicating potential risks. Predictive analytics models evaluate historical patterns and current data to identify early indicators of potential market slowdowns, tenant default risks, and economic downturns. Investors can predict market demand changes by using consumer spending data alongside interest rate and employment rate information, which allows them to modify their investment portfolios as needed.

Through data analytics, investors can predict market corrections when rental prices in particular cities show unsustainable growth patterns. The acquired knowledge enables investors to distribute their investments among different markets and secure favorable leases or postpone buying properties until prices stabilize. Through market change predictions, investors can reduce financial risks and stay clear of excessively leveraged investments.

Let's look at this example:

Mark, an experienced real estate investor, developed his rental property portfolio to span multiple major urban areas. Throughout his career, he used standard investment approaches, which consisted of market intuition and historical performance analysis, to make his investment choices. When housing prices in his primary investment city, Austin, Texas, began to surge, Mark chose to adopt big data and predictive analytics in his strategy to determine if the real estate boom could continue.

Mark's examination of predictive models, together with historical rental data, showed him that Austin rental prices were escalating faster than local income and employment statistics would allow. The analysis showed that fewer people were moving to the area while the vacancy rates for new developments increased. Economic indicators showed potential growth in interest rates, which would decrease both housing affordability and market demand. Mark decided to delay purchasing new properties in Austin and shifted his investment focus towards secondary markets, which demonstrated stable expansion and stronger economic foundations.

The market correction Mark predicted happened after several months when property values stopped growing, and rental rates dropped because of an oversupply and diminishing demand. Thanks to his data-driven risk reduction strategy, Mark avoided financial losses during the market downturn, which affected over-leveraged investors. Using significant data forecasting to identify early warning signs allowed him to avoid an overheated market while making investments in regions with steady long-term appreciation, which demonstrated that strategic decision-making supported by data is essential for risk management and investment success (Maximizing Profits).

Optimizing Pricing and Rental Strategies:

Big data is also reshaping how investors determine optimal rental and home sales pricing. Major rental platforms like Airbnb and Zillow utilize dynamic pricing algorithms that modify rates by analyzing seasonal trends, local competition, and tenant demand. Landlords who adapt their pricing strategies to reflect current market conditions and maintain competitive rates can achieve maximum rental income.

Landlords use big data analysis of rental yield to establish rent prices that optimize profitability and occupancy rates. Data-driven pricing models evaluate tenant income levels, crime rates, walkability scores, and nearby property values to ensure that properties remain attractive to renters and offer good returns to investors.

Let's look at Sophia, who had extensive real estate investment experience and multiple short-term rental properties in Miami, Florida. Her properties demonstrated strong historical performance, but she also observed seasonal variations in occupancy rates and rental income fluctuations. To achieve maximum profitability alongside high occupancy rates, she adopted big data-driven pricing strategies to fine-tune her rental prices.

Sophia programmed her rental properties to link with a dynamic pricing platform that tracked seasonal demand and local events while comparing competitor rates. The system automatically changed her rental prices at all times so she could demand top rates during high-demand tourist periods and set attractive prices during quiet months to sustain occupancy. Her properties generated 15% more annual rental income because dynamic pricing drew customers who paid premium rates.

Sophia expanded her application of big data rental yield analysis to include one of her long-term rental properties. Sophia used data-driven tools to review tenant income trends alongside neighborhood crime rates and walkability scores to find the best rent price. Her rental rate strategy matched tenant financial capacity and market needs, which resulted in both minimal vacancies and maximized rental revenue. Her investments stayed profitable and competitive while maintaining sustainability because she relied on data-driven strategies in an ever-changing market.

AI-Powered Tenant Screening and Portfolio Management:

The use of big data extends beyond market analysis to include essential functions in tenant selection and risk reduction. AI-powered screening tools allow landlords to evaluate rental candidates by examining their rental history alongside financial habits and credit scores, as well as social media activity for creditworthiness. Landlords can reduce delayed payments and property damage risks while improving cash flow through big data tenant screening, which also decreases tenant turnover rates.

AI-based asset management platforms enable investors with diverse property portfolios to monitor property performance and evaluate expense ratios and maintenance costs. Investors utilize real-time dashboards from these tools to identify properties that perform poorly and forecast maintenance needs while enhancing operational efficiency across several properties.

Future-Proofing Investment Strategies:

The evolving real estate markets will place increasing importance on big data. Investors who embrace data analytics, machine learning, and predictive modeling will have a distinct advantage in identifying high-growth opportunities, mitigating risks, and maximizing returns. Additionally, as blockchain technology and alternative data sources (e.g., mobile location tracking and consumer spending habits) become more integrated into real estate analytics, the ability to make highly precise, forward-looking investment decisions will only increase.

So, we see that big data has transformed real estate investment strategies by delivering unmatched insights that enable investors to make informed decisions based on solid data evidence (Understanding Big Data Analytics...). Real estate professionals who use real-time market analysis, predictive analytics, geospatial tools, and AI-driven pricing models can minimize investment risks while optimizing property prices and recognizing new market trends early. Real estate firms that apply significant data capabilities will sustain success and adaptability against intense competition within the ever-changing industry.

Practical market analysis in real estate investing requires access to multiple data sources. Investors who succeed in market analysis acquire their insights by merging property database data with government reports, rental platform information, and economic indicators. Investors who analyze data from various sources create more precise forecasting models that minimize unexpected downturn risks alongside forecast errors.

Geospatial and Location-Based Data for Investment Strategy:

Location continues to be fundamental to real estate success, but advanced geospatial analytics enable investors to evaluate neighborhoods and property potential with enhanced accuracy. Traditional methods of location analysis depended on examining broad market patterns and historical sales information. Modern Geographic Information Systems (GIS) and heat maps deliver real-time data-driven insights that help investors make strategic decisions.

Investors can use GIS technology to incorporate various data layers, such as infrastructure progress and public transport access, while considering crime statistics and school performance to evaluate neighborhood potential beyond traditional sales records. Through detailed examination, investors can determine which markets are growing while others remain stagnant. Neighborhoods that experience new business openings, better transit access, and increased pedestrian activity typically demonstrate future residential and commercial property demand. Investors who utilize this information can secure early-stage prospects before property values rise substantially.

Location-based information improves risk evaluation by pinpointing potential investment dangers, including flood areas and environmental and socio-economic changes that may affect property values. Geospatial mapping and predictive analytics reveal urban development patterns alongside gentrification and planned government infrastructure projects. Investors can fine-tune their investment strategies through this data-driven approach by choosing properties in high-growth, low-risk areas that meet short-term rental income goals and long-term appreciation expectations. Real estate investors who adopt geospatial technology into their decision-making process achieve a competitive edge when choosing profitable and sustainable property investments.

Geospatial analytics enables precise identification of regions that are currently experiencing infrastructure development and urban renewal. Investors can analyze public records and city planning data to determine where new highways, bridges, subway lines, or commercial centers are being built factors that typically drive property appreciation. The construction of a new public transportation hub can stimulate demand for adjacent residential and commercial properties, which will result in increased rental yields and higher resale values.

GIS technology lets investors evaluate walkability scores and proximity to essential facilities like schools and hospitals, along with shopping centers and entertainment districts beyond large infrastructure projects (Navigating the Journey...). Properties in high walkability zones often attract tenants and buyers seeking convenience, increasing occupancy rates and property valuations.

Real-Time Traffic and Mobility Insights:

Today's real estate investors utilize real-time traffic information to evaluate how easily people can access locations and understand travel patterns. Using AI, Mobility tracking systems evaluate vehicle and pedestrian movements to identify congested areas and efficient travel routes. The analysis of foot traffic patterns provides essential data to predict successful commercial investments in retail spaces, restaurants, and office buildings.

Additionally, rideshare data (Uber, Lyft, etc.) The data on public transit usage rates gives a more detailed understanding of transportation patterns. Investors can pinpoint locations where demand for housing may increase due to improved commuting conditions or rising remote work trends that shift demand toward suburban areas.

Demographic and Economic Trends for Long-Term Appreciation:

Geospatial analytics also helps investors track shifting demographic patterns and job market trends, which are critical for forecasting long-term property appreciation. AI-powered GIS platforms can aggregate census data, migration trends, and economic growth indicators to highlight areas experiencing population booms or economic revitalization.

For example, suppose a previously declining neighborhood starts attracting an influx of young professionals due to the opening of a new business district. If these conditions persist, investors should expect a housing market with greater demand, which will lead to higher property values. When data shows employment decline and outward migration patterns, investors will stop buying property and will need to update their pricing models.

Geospatial analytics defends investor assets by mapping out environmental dangers paired with zoning limitations and climate risks while conducting growth potential evaluations. AI mapping tools help investors locate properties in regions prone to flooding and earthquakes, along with areas with high insurance costs caused by climate risks. Through the integration of environmental data into their decision-making processes, investors gain the ability to assess long-term sustainability risks and make necessary adjustments to their investment strategies.

Modern investors who employ advanced geospatial analytics, heat maps, and real-time location intelligence achieve better property selection and market forecasting capabilities. Real-time location intelligence tools offer investors a complete data-based understanding of location-based investments throughout various stages, from infrastructure development to population changes. Through real-time geographic insights, investors can better identify high-growth regions while optimizing pricing strategies and reducing location risks. This results in more informed decision-making within the dynamic real estate sector.

Risk Management Through AI and Machine Learning:

Investors use AI models to assess risks associated with property acquisition by studying historical market fluctuations, mortgage default rates, and local vacancy trends. Machine learning algorithms enable these models to process enormous datasets and discover complicated patterns beyond human analytical capability. AI analyzes previous market cycles along with socio-economic data to predict whether a market will experience growth, stability, or decline. Investors receive critical intelligence through data analysis, which informs their property investment choices to buy, hold, or sell.

AI-driven predictive analytics provides crucial value through its capability to identify early indicators of property value declines and economic instability. Local vacancy rate spikes, together with rising mortgage delinquencies and regional job growth deceleration, can serve as indicators of market softening. AI models provide real-time monitoring and updates on indicators, which enable investors to obtain immediate risk assessments. Investors should move their capital to stable or high-growth areas to diversify their portfolios before market conditions worsen.

AI-driven risk models assist investors in developing pricing strategies by predicting future rental yields and property values. These models use rent growth patterns alongside consumer behavior analysis and demand-supply imbalances to determine competitive real estate pricing that maximizes investment returns. This ensures that investors do not overprice units, risk extended vacancies, or underprice properties and miss out on potential profits.

AI also enhances risk management by integrating climate and environmental risk analysis into investment decisions. The analysis of past weather patterns, along with flood zones and natural disaster probabilities through machine learning algorithms, helps predict ecological risks that may affect a property's long-term value. Risk assessments created by AI deliver essential information for predicting insurance expenses and planning company sustainability efforts for investors considering properties in coastal regions or areas prone to wildfires.

Furthermore, AI models refine tenant quality assessments by analyzing historical rental payment behaviors, credit history, and even online reviews of rental properties. Landlords and property managers can use this system to spot low-risk tenants who tend to pay their rent on time and look after their properties, which reduces operational risks over time.

Investors who utilize AI-driven risk assessment tools achieve advanced data-supported methods to handle uncertainties within real estate markets. AI improves investors' strategic decision-making ability through emerging risk identification and pricing model optimization while predicting market shifts, thereby maintaining portfolio resilience during economic fluctuations.

Guidelines for Effective Use of Data Analytics:

While big data provides powerful insights, human oversight remains critical. Investors should routinely verify data accuracy, track how economic shifts affect long-term property performance, and avoid over-relying on automated forecasts without contextual market knowledge. A structured approach that blends data-driven strategies with on-the-ground research results in better decision-making.

The Influence of Virtual Tours and AI in Marketing:

Modern real estate marketing depends on virtual and AI-driven tools because technology has transformed property marketing practices. Especially when it comes to international investing. Virtual tours transformed property presentations by allowing investors to connect with global buyers and renters free from physical location limits.

Three main virtual tour formats exist for showcasing properties.

360-degree photo walk-throughs provide panoramic views of real estate properties.

Interactive Virtual Reality experiences give the users full immersion capabilities for property navigation.

Augmented Reality (AR) overlays enable potential buyers to preview renovation possibilities, furniture arrangements, and design modifications before making a purchase.

The implementation of proper lighting and interactive features in virtual tours, combined with seamless navigation, boosts user interaction while driving higher conversion rates.

AI Bias and Ethical Considerations:

The increasing use of AI in real estate marketing brings forward critical issues about algorithmic bias that need resolution. The use of historical user behavior data by AI property recommendation engines results in the unintentional reinforcement of neighborhood selection biases. Human supervision continues to be essential for operating these AI systems, as previously discussed. The consistent evaluation of AI marketing systems prevents discriminatory advertising while maintaining equitable practices in property marketing.

Data-driven exclusion remains a critical issue, as AI-enabled real estate platforms potentially lead buyers and renters away from particular neighborhoods through analysis of their previous search patterns. AI systems that identify users from specific demographics or income levels favoring certain neighborhoods may overlook listings in diverse or developing areas, thus restricting investment and purchasing possibilities for buyers and investors. Real estate experts, alongside technology developers, need to establish bias detection methods, maintain routine audits on AI training data, and implement fair housing compliance systems to align AI property suggestions with established ethical and legal norms.

AI applications in property pricing predictions and loan approval processes raise ethical questions about equitable access to housing. AI models that depend excessively on historical lending patterns and obsolete credit models risk creating systemic inequality by decreasing mortgage approvals in communities that have experienced historical financial neglect. To prevent digital redlining, developers must ensure AI transparency and utilize diverse datasets while regulatory bodies maintain oversight. The real estate sector can achieve AI efficiency and fairness through human supervision and ongoing algorithmic assessments, leading to equitable housing opportunities.

AI-Powered Predictive Marketing and Customer Insights:

Real estate professionals use AI-driven insights from user preferences and browsing behavior to develop customized property suggestions, which enable them to adapt their marketing strategies to the unique requirements of individual buyers. AI algorithms can enhance property recommendations by monitoring user interaction patterns with listings, including viewed property types and price range preferences, to display listings that meet buyers' specific requirements. When buyers receive personalized suggestions, they are more inclined to engage, which results in quicker transaction completion and higher customer satisfaction levels.

Predictive lead scoring takes AI-driven marketing a step further by assessing the probability of a prospective buyer making a purchase based on their behavior and previous interactions. AI models analyze various data points, including website visit frequency, specific listing engagement time, historical agent communications, and promotional campaign responses. Real estate specialists can focus on leads with high purchasing potential while minimizing the time used on less engaged prospects through this prioritization process. Predictive lead scoring streamlines sales while optimizing resource allocation, enhancing marketing success rates, and increasing operational efficiency.

AI-powered customer support chatbots enhance user engagement through immediate access to information around the clock while removing lengthy wait periods and delivering information to prospective buyers when they need it most. Chatbots allow users to receive quick answers about listings, book property visits, and get mortgage estimates, which leads to a smooth experience for users. Advanced AI virtual assistants analyze conversation history and context to create more relevant, human-like user interactions. When real estate firms connect chatbots to CRM systems, they establish better lead management through conversation tracking and enable consistent buyer communication. The automation system boosts customer satisfaction because it allows agents to focus on complex client interactions, leading to enhanced productivity and better sales results.

Virtual Staging for Enhanced Listings:

As an AI-driven feature, virtual staging serves as a modern and economical property marketing solution, replacing conventional staging methods. Virtual staging employs advanced rendering technology to digitally furnish vacant properties and create visually appealing photorealistic interiors instead of requiring furniture rentals, designer hiring, and logistical arrangements needed for physical staging. Real estate professionals can display properties in their best condition without the high costs and time investments required for conventional staging methods.

Virtual staging stands out because it delivers various design options to attract multiple buyer demographics. For instance, a property can be digitally staged in a contemporary minimalist style for younger buyers, a classic design for more traditional buyers, or even a home office setup for professionals seeking work-from-home options. The ability to customize spaces lets buyers see how properties will fit their particular lifestyle requirements, which helps them form an emotional connection to the property.

The newest virtual staging tools powered by AI technology now include augmented reality features that enable buyers to experience staged environments through real-time interaction. Potential buyers can utilize AR applications to tour a staged home virtually, switch furniture items, alter color schemes, and view potential renovation outcomes before completing their purchase. The interactive features of virtual staging tools deliver customized experiences that boost buyer engagement by offering creative control and enhancing their confidence in making purchase decisions.

Beyond marketing benefits, virtual staging also plays a crucial role in online property listings. Since most buyers begin their home search online, high-quality, well-staged images significantly increase click-through rates and listing engagement. Real estate listings with attractive virtual staging receive more inquiries and generate increased interest than properties featuring vacant or unappealing interiors. Through the application of AI-driven virtual staging techniques, real estate agents achieve standout listings, which lead to quicker sales transactions and peak property values. Real estate technology continues to advance while new innovations emerge for the future. Investors must remain flexible and actively embrace new tools as real estate technology evolves.

Adapting to Rapid Technological Change:

Rapid advancements in PropTech require investors to establish ongoing learning strategies. Businesses maintain their competitive edge in digital markets by attending industry conferences, forming partnerships with technology firms, and providing continuous software training programs. Real estate professionals can use periodic technology audits to determine if their current tools maintain effectiveness or require upgrades.

Blockchain technology will revolutionize real estate transactions through its secure and transparent property ownership verification system that maintains tamper-proof records for easy access. Blockchain technology uses decentralized ledgers to remove the requirement of traditional third-party checks from banks and governmental bodies, thereby speeding up transactions and reducing expenses. This transparency reduces the risk of fraud, ownership disputes, and forged documents, as every transaction is recorded in a publicly accessible and immutable ledger.

One of the most transformative applications of blockchain in real estate is the application of smart contracts self-executing digital agreements that are programmed to trigger actions automatically once predefined conditions are met. These contracts remove intermediary requirements, which leads to lower transaction costs, faster processing times, and reduced risk of errors or disputes (Future of Fintech). Smart contracts enable the automatic transfer of ownership rights, and funds release between buyer and seller when property sale conditions like inspection approvals and mortgage funding are met (The Rise of NFTs). The automation delivered by this system results in transactions that run smoothly and securely while speeding up the process.

Property deed verification and title management benefit from blockchain technology, which addresses historical inefficiencies, fraudulent activities, and clerical errors. The manual verification of paper-based title records is time-consuming and often leads to prolonged closing times and disputes. Real estate professionals can maintain secure property ownership records through blockchain-based digital title storage, enabling straightforward historical verification. Permanent maintenance and accessibility of property records minimize legal disputes and speed up title transfer processes.

Beyond domestic transactions, blockchain is revolutionizing cross-border real estate investments, allowing global investors to securely buy, sell, and manage properties with greater ease. Through tokenization, property ownership is divided into blockchain-based digital tokens real estate assets can be fractionally owned, enabling investors to buy smaller shares of high-value properties. By allowing the trading of property tokens on blockchain platforms, this innovation enhances market liquidity because it removes traditional real estate ownership constraints like geographic limitations and long holding periods.

Blockchain technology allows secure rental agreements while maintaining efficient execution because smart contracts make lease terms transparent. Cryptocurrency and blockchain-linked digital payments allow for automated rent payments, which solve late payment problems and remove third-party transaction costs. Access to rental histories for both tenants and landlords enhances trust-building while streamlining tenant screening processes.

With these advancements, blockchain technology is set to reshape the real estate industry by offering a decentralized, secure, and efficient alternative to conventional property transactions. As adoption increases, investors and industry professionals who integrate blockchain solutions into their business models will gain a more competitive edge by streamlining operations, reducing costs, and enhancing transaction security.

Sustainability and Green Technology in Real Estate:

The sustainability movement has driven the adoption of smart energy systems and sustainable building materials across various sectors. Investors who adopt green technology applications such as solar software optimization and automated energy tracking systems achieve financial success over time and gain environmental benefits.

Sustainable real estate practices not only cut operational expenses but also boost property value while drawing in tenants and buyers who prioritize environmental responsibility. In the real estate industry, green certifications like LEED and Energy Star ratings now serve as major distinguishing factors that show potential occupants that properties meet top-tier efficiency and environmental performance standards. Property owners who adopt renewable energy solutions and efficient water systems receive financial support from governments worldwide through tax benefits and grants. Financial incentives enable investors to recover initial costs, which makes sustainable property improvements both attainable and financially rewarding.

Progress in green building materials technology is transforming traditional methods of construction and property renovation. Buildings constructed with low-carbon concrete, recycled steel, and biodegradable insulation materials achieve reduced environmental impact alongside sustained durability and performance. Smart home automation systems, including AI-powered climate control and adaptive lighting solutions, improve energy efficiency by adapting to usage patterns and environmental conditions. Real estate investors who adopt sustainable technologies create long-term financial benefits and protect their properties against future regulation changes and shifting consumer demands. This secures their market position and investment achievements in today's eco-aware environment.

The Concluding Thoughts:

Real estate investing has undergone a fundamental transformation through technology, which enables investors to manage properties more efficiently while assessing risks and marketing listings. The utilization of AI-driven analysis and blockchain transactions helps maintain competitive advantages for sustained success. Automation enhances operational efficiency while human expertise remains indispensable for data interpretation, deal negotiation, and delivering personalized customer service.

Real estate professionals must maintain flexibility in response to technological advancements by adopting suitable new tools that support their investment approaches. By embracing innovation while maintaining ethical standards and data security, investors can build resilient, future-proof businesses in an increasingly digital landscape.

Document Management System for Real Estate. https://myeoffice.in/document-management-system-for-real-estate/

Maximizing Profits: The Impact of Data Warehouse Consulting Services on Your Bottom Line - Wisto Weekly. https://wistoweekly.com/maximizing-profits-the-impact-of-data-warehouse-consulting-services-on-your-bottom-line

Understanding Big Data Analytics with an Innovation Speaker's Help.

https://www.thedigitalspeaker.com/understanding-big-data-analytics-innovation-speaker-help/

Navigating the Journey: A Guide for Home Buyers and Sellers – Count Down to Pregnancy. https://countdowntopregnancy.net/navigating-the-journey-a-guide-for-home-buyers-and-sellers/

Future of Fintech: Trends, Innovations & Growth | The Connector.. https://www.jointheconnector.com/post/the-future-of-fintech-trends-innovations-and-growth-opportunities

The Rise of NFTs: What They Are and How They Work - Harmony Hustle. https://harmonyhustle.com/2023/04/25/the-rise-of-nfts-what-they-are-and-how-they-work/

Conclusion

From First Deal to Global Vision: Your Journey Starts Here

Whether you're just beginning your real estate journey or standing at the edge of international opportunity, one truth remains: the future of real estate investing belongs to the creative.

The world of real estate investing is often framed by limitations credit barriers, financial shortfalls, or rigid lending criteria. Yet, as this book has shown, those limitations are not walls; they are merely challenges that can be navigated with the right mindset and the right tools. Creative financing is not just a collection of alternative funding techniques. It is a philosophy of resourcefulness, resilience, and strategic action.

This book aims to empower you to take action and redefine your role as both a borrower and investor through strategic thinking. The ability to unlock value in every deal exists because each property represents a complex puzzle that others perceive as merely complicated. After mastering the principles outlined in these pages and forming the right partnerships through careful planning, you now possess the necessary clarity and confidence to move ahead.

For first-time investors, the idea of acquiring property may feel distant, as it may be blocked by credit challenges, limited capital, or fear of making the wrong move. But as you've discovered in this book, creative financing opens doors where traditional methods shut them down. You don't need perfect credit, deep pockets, or approval from a conventional lender. You need a strategy, a willingness to learn, and the courage to act. Every chapter in this book has provided you with tools to start from wherever you are with seller financing, lease options, subject-to-deals, and other techniques that turn ambition into achievement.

For the global investor, creative financing extends far beyond local deals. It offers a blueprint for thinking bigger about cross-border investments, currency-conscious financing structures, and building a resilient, diversified portfolio. The international real estate market is rich with opportunities for those who understand the risks, research the landscape, and move with strategic intent. Whether you're eyeing rental properties in emerging economies or stable returns in foreign cities, you now possess the framework to explore and engage with markets worldwide.

You have now explored an array of proven, non-traditional strategies: seller financing, lease options, private lending, subject-to-deals, and more. You've learned how to evaluate opportunities, structure deals creatively, manage risk, and even look beyond national borders to tap into the potential of international real estate markets. You've also gained insights into the importance of mentorship, the use of data and technology, and the value of long-term, cash-flow-driven thinking.

More importantly, you've seen that success in real estate investing doesn't depend on a perfect financial résumé it depends on how creatively and confidently you respond to obstacles. Whether you are just beginning your investment journey or scaling an existing portfolio, creative financing gives you the flexibility to grow on your terms. Creative financing is more than a method; it's a mindset. It asks you to see potential where others see limitation, to adapt when conditions shift, and to act with both prudence and purpose. You've now been equipped with the insights, models, and examples that can reshape your financial future one smart deal at a time.

Let this be more than a learning experience let it be your launching point.   But knowledge alone doesn't build empires action does. No matter your stage or scope, this truth applies: knowledge alone doesn't build wealth applied knowledge does.

So, what's next?
•   If this is your first step, take it boldly. Find that first property, run the numbers, make the offer, and learn by doing.
•   If you're looking globally, engage experts, study foreign markets, and explore deals that align with your long-term vision.

You have everything you need to begin or begin again armed not just with tactics but with the confidence that creative investors can thrive in any market   under   any   conditions. This isn't the end of the book. It's the start of your next   chapter.
Move forward. Think creatively. Act decisively. The world of real estate is now open to you locally and globally.

A Final Note from the Author

Thank you for taking the time to read this book. I truly hope the insights and strategies shared within these pages have been both informative and empowering for your journey.

If you found this book valuable, I would deeply appreciate it if you could leave a brief review. Your feedback not only helps others discover this resource, but it also supports the continued development of future content that serves readers like you.

You can leave your review here:

☞
https://www.amazon.com/dp/B0F4T4LPWL?ref_=pe_93986420_775043100

With sincere gratitude,

John Workman, Ph.D.

Appendix A: Key Terms & Definitions

Understanding the terminology of real estate and creative financing is essential for success. Below is a list of key terms used throughout this book:

• Creative Financing – Non-traditional methods of financing real estate purchases, including seller financing, lease options, private lending, and more.

• Seller Financing – A financing arrangement where the property seller acts as the lender, allowing the buyer to make payments directly to them instead of a traditional bank.

• Lease Option – A contract that allows a tenant to rent a property with the option to purchase it later, often at a predetermined price.

• Private Money Lender – An individual or private entity that provides real estate financing without going through traditional banking institutions.

• Debt-to-Income Ratio (DTI) – A financial metric that compares an investor's monthly debt obligations to their monthly income, used by lenders to assess loan eligibility.

• Loan-to-Value Ratio (LTV) – A percentage comparing the loan amount to the appraised value of a property; the lower the LTV, the less risk for the lender.

- Hard Money Loan – A short-term, asset-based loan typically used by real estate investors to acquire and renovate properties quickly.

- Equity – The difference between a property's market value and the amount owed on its mortgage; an investor's ownership stake in the property.

- Cash Flow – The net income generated from a rental property after deducting all operating expenses and mortgage payments.

- Cap Rate (Capitalization Rate) – A metric used to evaluate the return on investment of a rental property, calculated by dividing net operating income (NOI) by the property's purchase price or value.

- Debt Service Coverage Ratio (DSCR) – A financial ratio that compares a property's net operating income to its debt obligations, used to assess an investor's ability to cover loan payments.

- Subject-To Financing – A method where an investor takes over the existing mortgage payments of a property while keeping the loan in the original owner's name.

Appendix B: Creative Financing Strategies at a Glance

This section provides a quick reference guide to different creative financing strategies covered in the book.

Appendix C: International Real Estate Investment Considerations

For those looking to invest in real estate globally, here are some key factors to consider:

• Foreign Investment Laws – Each country has unique regulations on foreign property ownership. Research restrictions and legal frameworks before investing.

• Currency Exchange Risks – Fluctuations in exchange rates can impact property values and investment returns. Consider using currency hedging strategies.

• Financing Challenges – Traditional mortgage lenders may not offer loans to foreign investors. Explore local financing options, private lending, or partnerships.

• Tax Implications – Understanding local and international tax laws is crucial for managing investment returns. Some countries impose additional taxes on foreign investors.

- Market Research – Assess economic stability, property appreciation trends, and rental demand before entering a foreign market.

- Legal and Title Risks – Some regions may have complex land ownership laws. Work with a local real estate attorney to ensure a clear and secure title.

Appendix D: Recommended Resources

To deepen your knowledge of creative financing and real estate investing, consider the following resources:

Books & Publications:
- The Millionaire Real Estate Investor – Gary Keller
- Rich Dad Poor Dad – Robert Kiyosaki
- Investing in Apartment Buildings – Matthew A. Martinez
- The Book on Rental Property Investing – Brandon Turner

Online Platforms & Websites:
- BiggerPockets (www.biggerpockets.com) – A leading real estate investing community with forums, blogs, and educational materials.
- Investopedia (www.investopedia.com) – Provides definitions and articles on financial and investment concepts.
- U.S. Department of Housing and Urban Development (www.hud.gov) – Government resource for real estate financing programs and

regulations.
• Foreign Property Investment Guides (various websites by country) – Check official government investment portals for country-specific information.

Networking & Investment Groups:
• National Real Estate Investors Association (www.nationalreia.org)
• International Real Estate Federation (www.fiabci.org)
• Local real estate investment meetups and Facebook groups

Appendix E: Sample Contracts & Forms

For those new to creative financing, here are some basic contract templates to review with a real estate attorney before use:
• Sample Seller Financing Agreement
• Sample Lease Option Agreement
• Sample Hard Money Loan Promissory Note
• Sample Joint Venture Agreement for Real Estate Partnerships
Disclaimer: These sample documents are for educational purposes only. Always consult a qualified attorney before signing any real estate contract.

Appendix F: Common Myths & Misconceptions About Creative Financing

Many investors hesitate to use creative financing due to common misconceptions. Below are myths debunked:

Myth: Creative financing is only for people with bad credit.
Reality: Many seasoned investors use creative financing to leverage their investments, preserve cash flow, and scale their portfolios efficiently.

Myth: Seller financing is risky for sellers.
Reality: When structured correctly with clear terms, seller financing can benefit both parties, often providing sellers with a steady income and higher returns.

Myth: You can't invest in real estate without a traditional mortgage.
Reality: Many investors acquire properties without conventional bank loans using seller financing, lease options, and private lending.

Myth: International real estate investing is too complicated.
Reality: While foreign markets present unique challenges, they also offer great opportunities. With proper research, local legal guidance, and strategic financing, investing abroad can be highly profitable.

Final   Thoughts:
The world of real estate investing is evolving, and
creative financing is at the forefront of this change.
Whether you are leveraging seller financing,
securing properties through lease options, or
expanding into global markets, the knowledge in
this book will serve as your foundation for success.

By using this appendix as a reference guide, you'll
be equipped with the terminology, strategies, and
resources to confidently navigate real estate
investing in any market.

Glossary of Terms

This glossary provides definitions of key terms and
concepts related to creative financing and real
estate investing. Use this as a reference to deepen
your understanding of the strategies and financial
principles   discussed   in   this   book.

A
•   Adjustable-Rate   Mortgage   (ARM):   A
mortgage with an interest rate that changes
periodically based on an index, causing payments
to   fluctuate   over   time.
•   Amortization: The process of gradually
paying off a loan through regular payments that
cover   both   interest   and   principal.
•   Appraisal: A professional evaluation of a
property's market value, usually conducted by a
licensed   appraiser.
•   Asset-Based Lending: A type of loan where
the borrower's assets (such as real estate) serve as

collateral rather than relying solely on creditworthiness.

B

•   Balloon Payment: A large, lump-sum payment due at the end of a loan term, often found in seller financing or certain types of mortgages.
•   Bridge Loan: A short-term loan used to finance a real estate purchase until permanent financing is secured or an existing property is sold.
•   Buy-and-Hold Strategy: A long-term investment approach where an investor purchases a property to rent it out for consistent cash flow and   appreciation.

C

•   Cap Rate (Capitalization Rate): A formula used to evaluate the return on investment for a rental property, calculated by dividing net operating income (NOI) by the purchase price or market   value.
•   Cash Flow: The net income generated from a rental property after deducting all expenses, including mortgage payments, taxes, and maintenance.
•   Closing Costs: Fees and expenses paid at the end of a real estate transaction, including title insurance, loan origination fees, and legal fees.
•   Collateral: An asset pledged as security for a loan, which can be seized if the borrower defaults.
•   Crowdfunding: A method of raising capital for real estate projects by pooling funds from multiple investors through online platforms.

D

- Debt Service: The total amount required to cover loan payments, including principal and interest.
- Debt Service Coverage Ratio (DSCR): A financial metric that compares a property's net operating income to its debt obligations, indicating whether the property generates enough income to cover its loan payments.
- Deed-in-Lieu of Foreclosure: An agreement where a borrower voluntarily transfers property ownership to the lender to avoid foreclosure.
- Depreciation: A tax deduction that accounts for the reduction in value of a property over time due to wear and tear.

E

- Equity: The difference between a property's market value and the amount owed on its mortgage; an investor's ownership stake in the property.
- Escrow: A neutral third-party account where funds are held until all conditions of a real estate transaction are met.
- Exit Strategy: A planned method for an investor to sell or transition out of an investment, such as selling a property, refinancing, or using a lease option.

F

- Fix-and-Flip: A short-term investment strategy where a property is purchased, renovated, and resold for profit.
- Foreclosure: The legal process where a

lender seizes and sells a property due to a borrower's failure to make loan payments.
• Forbearance: A temporary agreement between a lender and borrower to reduce or pause mortgage payments due to financial hardship.

G
• Gross Rental Income: The total income a property generates from rent before deducting expenses.
• Ground Lease: A lease agreement where a tenant rents land but is responsible for building and maintaining structures on it.
• Guarantor: A person or entity that agrees to be responsible for a loan if the borrower defaults.

H
• Hard Money Loan: A short-term, high-interest loan provided by private lenders based on the value of a property rather than the borrower's creditworthiness.
• HELOC (Home Equity Line of Credit): A revolving credit line secured by the equity in a borrower's property.
• Holding Costs: Expenses incurred while owning a property, including mortgage payments, taxes, insurance, and maintenance.

I
• Interest-Only Loan: A loan where the borrower only pays interest for a specified period before starting to repay the principal.
• International Real Estate Investing: The practice of purchasing and managing properties in

foreign markets for diversification and financial growth.

• Investment Property: Real estate purchased with the intention of generating rental income, appreciation, or both.

J

• Joint Venture (JV): A partnership between two or more investors who pool resources to acquire and manage a property while sharing profits and risks.

L

• Lease Option: An agreement where a tenant rents a property with the right to purchase it at a predetermined price within a specified period.

• Lease Purchase: Similar to a lease option, but the tenant is contractually obligated to buy the property at the end of the lease term.

• Lien: A legal claim against a property as security for debt repayment, which must be settled before the property can be sold.

• Loan-to-Value Ratio (LTV): A percentage comparing the loan amount to the appraised value of a property; lower LTVs indicate lower lender risk.

M

• Mortgage Note: A legal document outlining the terms of a loan, including the repayment schedule, interest rate, and consequences of default.

• Multi-Family Property: A building with multiple residential units, such as a duplex, triplex, or apartment complex, typically used for rental income.

N

• Net Operating Income (NOI): The total income from a rental property after operating expenses are deducted, excluding mortgage payments and taxes.
• Non-Recourse Loan: A loan where the lender's ability to recover losses is limited to the property itself, with no claim on the borrower's other assets.

• Non-Qualified Mortgage (Non-QM) Loans are alternative mortgage products designed for borrowers who do not meet the strict criteria of traditional Qualified Mortgage (QM) loans. Unlike conventional loans, Non-QM loans offer flexible income verification, allow higher debt-to-income (DTI) ratios, and are accessible to borrowers with lower credit scores or non-traditional financial histories. These loans are commonly used by self-employed individuals, real estate investors, and foreign nationals who may not qualify for traditional financing. While they provide greater accessibility, Non-QM loans often come with higher interest rates and less favorable terms due to increased lender risk

O

• Owner Financing (Seller Financing): A financing arrangement where the property seller provides a loan to the buyer instead of a bank.

P

- Passive Income: Earnings generated from rental properties with minimal day-to-day management.
- Prepayment Penalty: A fee charged by lenders if a borrower pays off a loan before the agreed-upon term.
- Private Money Lending: Loans provided by individual investors or private entities instead of traditional financial institutions.
- Property Management: The operation, control, and oversight of rental properties, often handled by professional firms.

R
- Real Estate Investment Trust (REIT): A company that owns, operates, or finances income-producing real estate and allows investors to buy shares.
- Refinancing: Replacing an existing mortgage with a new loan, often to secure a better interest rate or access home equity.
- Rent-to-Own: A leasing arrangement where tenants have the option to purchase the property after a specified period.

S
- Seller Carryback: A form of seller financing where the seller acts as the lender and extends credit to the buyer.
- Short Sale: A sale where the lender agrees to accept less than the total mortgage balance to prevent foreclosure.
- Subject-To Financing: A financing method where an investor takes over a seller's mortgage payments while keeping the loan in the original

owner's   name.

T

•   Tax Lien: A government claim against a property   due   to   unpaid   taxes.
•   Title Search: A review of public records to confirm legal ownership of a property and check for   any   liens   or   encumbrances.
•   Turnkey Property: A fully renovated, tenant-occupied rental property sold to an investor   as   a   ready-to-go   investment.

V

•   Vacancy Rate: The percentage of rental units that are unoccupied at any given time.
•   VA Loan: A mortgage program for veterans and active military members, offering favorable terms   and   requiring   no   down   payment.

W

•   Wholesale Real Estate: A strategy where an investor contracts a property at a discount and assigns the contract to another buyer for a profit without   taking   ownership.
•   Wraparound Mortgage: A secondary financing method where the seller's existing mortgage remains in place while they finance an additional loan to the buyer.

Bibliography

Churchill Mortgage. (n.d.). Loan programs.

Mehta, S. (2023). Creative financing: Real estate strategies, types, and examples. PodBean Development.

MULTI HOME LOANS LLC. (n.d.). Flexible home financing solutions: Non-QM loans demystified for homebuyers.

Purdie, A. (n.d.). Planning archives. TopMarketWatch. (n.d.). Unlocking cash flow: How invoice factoring benefits businesses.

Vaughns, S. (2012). Open innovation implementation: Competitor pathways.

Webber, M. (2022). Understanding lender expectations for mortgage applications. RealtyBiz News.

Owner Financing. (n.d.). Owner financing explained.

RealtyBizNews. (2023). New FHA changes - again.

New Branch Real Estate Advisors. (n.d.). The CAP Rate.

Hubler. (n.d.). Capitalization rate explained.

Chen, L. (2021). Equity and Real Estate Wealth Building.

Churchill Mortgage – Loan Types. Retrieved from

Columbian. (n.d.). Home Improvement Loans.

Digital Commons @ Old Dominion University – Creative Finance Collection.

Gio Music. (n.d.). House-buying companies: Real case studies.

Homebase. (n.d.). Real estate syndication legalities.

Investopedia. (n.d.). Debt service coverage ratio (DSCR).

Keller, G. (2005). The Millionaire Real Estate Investor.

Kotuvo. (n.d.). Transaction templates and service contracting.

Kiyosaki, R. T. (2000). Rich Dad, Poor Dad.

Landon, M. (2021). Operating Expenses for Rental Properties.

Luminareia. (n.d.). Cash flow projections explained.

Martinez, M. (2008). Investing in Apartment Buildings.

McElroy, K. (n.d.). Real estate investing tutorials.

Mynd Management. (n.d.). Rental property automation tools.

National REIA. (n.d.). Investor education and community building.

Neomartek. (n.d.). Loan servicing platforms.

Podcasts: Joe Fairless Show, Wealth Formula Podcast, Real Estate Guys Radio.

REIA Meetups – Real estate investment groups and events.

Roofstock. (n.d.). Single-family investment properties.

Turner, B. (2014). The Book on Investing in Real Estate with No (and Low) Money Down.

Tyson, E., & Griswold, R. S. (2016). Real Estate Investing for Dummies.

WebRanked. (n.d.). Marketing tools for real estate investors.

World Bank. (n.d.). Doing Business Index.

Government & Institutional Reports

•   U.S. Department of Housing and Urban Development (HUD). "FHA Loan Requirements and Financing Programs."

•   Federal Housing Finance Agency (FHFA). "Understanding Loan-to-Value Ratios and Mortgage Risk." 2023.

•   International Real Estate Federation (FIABCI). "Global Real Estate Investment Trends and Risk Management." 2022.

Podcasts & Video Resources

- BiggerPockets Real Estate Podcast. Hosted by Brandon Turner & David Greene.
- The Real Estate Guys Radio Show. Hosted by Robert Helms & Russell Gray.
- Creative Real Estate Investing Podcast. Hosted by Joe Fairless.
- Wealth Formula Podcast. Hosted by Buck Joffrey.

This bibliography includes sources, references, and additional readings used throughout this book "Overcoming Credit Roadblocks: Building Your Real Estate Empire with Creative Funding". These resources provide further insights into real estate investing, creative financing strategies, and global investment opportunities.

This collection of resources supports the principles and strategies outlined in Overcoming Credit Roadblocks. Readers who want to dive deeper into real estate investing, creative financing, cash flow management, and international real estate opportunities. Hopefully, you will find valuable insights in these references.

www.ingramcontent.com/pod-product-compliance
Lightning Source LLC
Chambersburg PA
CBHW071600210326
41597CB00019B/3338